HIGHEST MOUNTAIN

SURVIVING THE 20TH CENTURY 1925-2000 AND BEYOND

WL Crum

authorHOUSE®

AuthorHouse™
1663 Liberty Drive
Bloomington, IN 47403
www.authorhouse.com
Phone: 1-800-839-8640

First published by AuthorHouse   12/8/2009

ISBN: 978-1-4490-4098-7 (e)
ISBN: 978-1-4490-4101-4 (sc)

Printed in the United States of America
Bloomington, Indiana

This book is printed on acid-free paper.

FORWARD

This is the story of my early years, beginning February 26th 1925, through to about 1950. It is said this period in time spawned "The Greatest Generation". I am not convinced of that, for it could also be termed the un-luckiest considering these years included the great depression of the thirties and the biggest and deadliest war of all time, WW II in the forties.

The twenties and thirties—depression years—were very lean, and with epidemics of Tuberculosis, Diphtheria, Infantile paralysis (Polio), Measles, life was somewhat hazardous for a kid growing up. There were no seat belts, safety glass, etc, in the autos either. There was lead paint and asbestos everywhere. There were no child safety or labor laws at all. No minimum wage. As children, we had to take our chances along with the adults.

The difficult experience's of these years is what prepared us for the more difficult forties and WW II, and subsequently to be named "The Greatest Generation". However, several hundred thousand youth's of this generation did not survive the forties, and so it could also be called "The unluckiest generation" .

I started writing this biography about thirty years ago, beginning with the story of my misadventures as a gunner in the 8th Army Air Force of WWII. I termed this experience MY LONGEST DAY, or EXPENDED. The longest day title came from a movie titled THE LONGEST DAY. A story about the invasion of the Normandy coast of France on June 6th, 1944, by Allied forces. There was something like ten thousand military men expended to make that landing. Well, the Air Force bomber fleets were invading the enemy coasts for over two years before this date, preparing the way for landing of the tank, artillery and infantry forces. The casualty numbers of the air crews and the slaughter of citizens on the ground were never told. Late in the war, January 28th, 1945 I became one of those casualties. So I first named this story MY LONGEST DAY. Then I renamed it EXPENDED. Both names were equally descriptive, so both were used.

Many years later, I wrote about the POW experience that followed being expended. And some years following that, I decided that for the benefit of my family, I should write about my beginning years. My parents never got around to telling us children about their early history and since they grew up in the late nineteenth century on the plains of Kansas, I imagine that their story could be very interesting in that theirs were the times of Indians, Buffalo Bill, Wyatt Earp and all of those wild people.

And so, I have included my whole life up until my marriage to my great wife Marian. I anticipate that I will one day continue writing about the years of married life, raising four fine kids, earning our keep, first with RCA in the early days of television, then with Lockheed Missile and Space Co beginning with the early days of satellites and space travel.

Another purpose of writing my story, I wish to convey my apologies to my family, my friends and co-workers, for being so tight-lipped, and secretive about my war time experience. The fact is, the experience of bombing from five miles up, at temperatures of thirty, forty degrees below zero, in a thin skinned primitive B24, wearing an electric heated suit, oxygen mask, parachute, maewest, fur lined boots and gloves, was a very traumatic time and I was very scared the whole six months that I was obliged to participate. (I could not believe that I had volunteered) I was left with a bad case of PTSD as it is called these days. In any case, I could not bring myself to talk about that experience to my friends or anyone until recent years when I have attended a group of ex-fly boys and ex-POW's, most of whom were B17 or B24 pilots or crew members, shot down over Europe in 1943, 44 and 45. We all had very similar war time experiences of survival and have learned to loosen up and discuss those extraordinary times

Unfortunately, almost all of my early year family and friends that I address in this book, have passed away. May their ghost's be listening?

I wish to pay tribute to the five men on my B24 crew, who did not survive that Sunday, January 28th, 1945, and therefore became part of the FORTY FIVE THOUSAND 8th Air Force casualty list.

WILLIAM T. FAIRCLOTH	ASN 0-769110
HARVEY R. MUSKRAT	ASN 0-466591
CHARLES H. SPIVEY	ASN 38172923
WILLIE G. POUNDS	ASN 34815202
DONALD G. JOHNSON	ASN 17143786

TABLE OF CONTENTS

CHAPTER I

YEARS 1925----1935

My first year of life began in my parent's home in Van Nuys California, February 26, 1925. Today, at the winter of my life, I feel like the cat with nine lives. Over the years, I have had some terribly close encounters, with an Angel watching over me from day one. The teen years she did double duty. Then WW II began. The good LORD himself was with me through those twenty eight months that I served in the Army Air Force. That period was/is, the highest mountain encountered in my life and I feel very blessed to have survived. All together, life has been one big learning experience, covering the years of the late horse and buggy days, through to space travel. Some of these experiences might be worth passing down.

Being an only son among seven girls is an experience in itself. Actually it was only six girls because one sister, Eva Mae, died of diphtheria a year before I was born. Also, my oldest sister, Mildred, married and was out of the house when I was very little. I was 2nd from the last born. I had one younger sister, Beverly Jean. The two of us were very close because we were only a year and one half apart. My mother, realizing we would be her last, tried her best to spoil us both. However, that was difficult, for those were lean years.

Mothers did not work out of the home those days. They were kept plenty busy raising a family since there was nothing automatic. The washing was done on a scrub board until electric motors brought the tub with the agitator. After washing, the clothes were put through a wringer mounted on the side of the tub, then hung, one by one on the clothes line in the sun to dry. No sun, no dry. The wringer part of the process was somewhat hazardous, requiring my mother's full attention. When feeding in the clothes, she had to let go at the proper time to avoid having her hands pulled into the two rollers. My right hand still bears the scars of playing chicken with that wringer

My mom did all of the cooking; kids did the dishes. Everything was time consuming. The milkman delivered several quarts of raw milk to the door; the iceman delivered ice for the ice box. Mom canned the fruit which she made last all year long, as well as baked our bread, pies and cakes. In the old farm tradition, my Dad took her in the car to town each Saturday, and they purchased five dollars worth of groceries. I can remember my Dad complaining about spending so much on groceries.

Jeanie & Bill 1929

Sister Georgia and Bill 1927

When the Great Depression hit, my dad was forced to go on WPA. It became <u>very</u> lean. I don't ever remember going hungry, but I don't ever remember having steak and eggs either. My mother raised a dozen chickens on the vacant lot next door, so the Sunday dinner treat was boiled chicken and dumplings. One of my very early impressions was helping my MOM pick a rooster from the bunch, catching it, wringing its neck until dead. Later that day, it was served on the dinner table.

My dad had a big Chandler touring car in my early days. I remember a family Sunday outing to the beach at Santa Monica. It was a long trip over the steep and winding Coast Mountain road called Beverly Glen. Arriving at the beach, my Dad drove right down on the sand, almost to the water's edge. After a big fire was built, Mom fixed hot dogs. Kids played in the surf, built sand castles in the sand, and got sunburned (no suntan lotions). When the sun went down, it was time to head home. Mom fixed me a bed on the backseat floorboards of the auto. I remember going to sleep listening to that old Chandler's differential growl when accelerating from a stop sign. There were not too many stop signs those days. There was not too much acceleration either, as 30, 35 MPH was cruising. This car had one piece of glass which was the windshield. Otherwise, it was all open air and very drafty. For foul weather, my dad stopped on the side of the road, pulled out some snap on side curtains from the tool storage trunk, and spent a frustrating half hour installing them.

I think that car came to an end when one year at Christmas time, the whole family went in it to Van Nuys Blvd. to pick out a Christmas tree. After finding a tree from one of the local sales lots, we returned to the car which was parked against the curb on Victory Blvd. My dad tied the tree on the curb-side running board while we kids crowded into the car. Mother was in the front seat, holding Jeannie on her lap. Everybody was happy to have a nice big Christmas tree. My dad finished tying on the tree, walked around the front of the car, climbed into the driver's seat and proceeded to start the engine. There was a minor backfire then WHOOSH there were flames under the car, down the curb right under the tree, and on down the street. We kids were terrified that we could lose our Christmas tree. We all bailed out, while Dad saved the Christmas tree.

I remember starting kindergarten at the Van Nuys Grammar School on Gilmore Street, two blocks from home. My mother dressed me up in short pants and walked me to school on the first day. I hated those short pants. And I wasn't too impressed with school either. Playing ring around the rosy, one of the kids couldn't hold it and peed all over the floor.

When I was in first grade, I had a very nice lady teacher named Mrs. Fox. She promoted me one grade. So now I was in a class with most kids six months to a year older than myself. I guess that was a good thing. When my younger sister started school, we walked the two blocks to and from school together, and I was big brother. One day a mean kid started something with us, and that night at home I told my older sister Georgia about it. She was in fifth or sixth grade and quite athletic. Next day she accompanied us on our walk to school. When this troublemaker made his appearance, she gave him a slap in the face and told him to butt out. That was fine except a few hours later this kid was waiting for me. When I rounded the corner of a building, we came face to face. He gave me a punch in the stomach. I never told my sister. SISTERS CANNOT ALWAYS DEFEND YOU!!

I always had a dog when I was growing up. That was another early unforgettable experience. The family had this black and white dog called Dusky. We lived on a corner lot. One of the streets was a busy one. There were often farmers with their mule-propelled hay wagons going down the street to I don't know where. Many model A Fords, which were considerably faster, buzzed up and down the street. Anyway one morning before school, the dog was run over and killed. The memory that lingers is that of all us kids, all dressed for school, standing in a circle around Dad in the vacant lot. He was laboring to get a hole deep enough to properly bury this dog. All we kids were crying—tears. This was my first experience with death.

Our next dog, whose name I can't remember, was sort of swiped by Jeannie and I. Walking home from school, we always stopped to play with this real friendly mutt who was lounging around in its owner's front yard. The dog started following us home each day, and later in the day the owner would come after him. This went on for a week or so until the owner gave up. We had a new dog.

I don't remember how long this dog lasted, but when I was six or seven years old we acquired a wired hair terrier pup. We named her Snooty. Jeannie and I played with this dog all day long. She was one of the kids. I had this dog until 1949, when I was twenty-four years old and married. She was 17 years old, deaf and nearly blind when we finally had her put to sleep.

My mother taught me many things about getting along in life. One of those things was about the "boogie Man." I might not be here if she hadn't. Apparently there have always been people who would molest little boys. My oldest sister, Mildred, was married and had a son Donn. A year and a half younger than me, he was the closest thing to a brother that I ever had. One evening when they were visiting, Donn and I were playing alongside this busy street (Haseltine) when a 1928 Dodge went by. I saw all these big sombreros inside. It was almost dark, but I could still see these great big hats through the big square windows, both front and backseats. There must have been six people packed in there, all with big hats. The car went past us about fifty feet and stopped and then backed up a few feet. A rear door opened. One of these big hats with a big fat Mexican under it emerged from the car and started towards Donn and me. This had to be the "boogie man" my mom had told me about. I started to run back onto our property. I yelled to Donn to follow, which he did. The big fat hombre turned around, walked back to the car, climbed in and drove off. BEWARE of the BOOGIEMAN!!

My great old overworked mother taught me many things. One thing she did not teach me about was girls. You would think that growing up with six sisters I would know all about girls. But my mother misled me on that one. Being from the Victorian era, she always told me to treat my girlfriends the way I would like my sisters to be treated. Much much later in life I learned, mostly the hard way, that this is very wrong. No girlfriend wants to be treated as a sister!!! It makes me sick to think of all the opportunities that I muffed.

My dad taught me a lot also--not about living but about work. Dad was a workaholic. He had to be to raise a family of seven. He was an early day electrician. He lost his own electrical contracting business in the early stages of the Great Depression. However, even while on WPA digging ditches or whatever, he was in demand from some of the ranchers to repair an irrigation pump motor or a chicken incubator or any of the numerous electric machines upon which everyone depended. Sometimes, I would go with him on one of these trouble calls and I would be the "gopher"—go for this and go for that. This is one way I learned, watching and listening to the conversations. Sometimes the pay would be in the product, as in the case of the incubator. This was at a big chicken ranch, so the pay for fixing the incubator was a dozen chicks, which we took home to raise. Another time I went with my dad on a Sunday to a barber's home that was being wired for lights and outlets. I got to do all the crawling under the house. For our service, Dad and I got free haircuts for many years, at the going rate of twenty-five cents each.

My dad taught me early on to keep my eyes and ears open and my mouth shut. To this day, I am a good listener and a bad talker. He never talked much about his early years. He was born in 1877 in a dirt floor, one-room homestead cabin in Strong City, Kansas. His father was a Civil War veteran, also a survivor of the infamous Andersonville prison. George Washington Crum gave up farming the Kansas prairie and became mayor of Strong City. He died a couple of years before I was born.

My Dad did tell me about justice in those days. One day in his youth, a couple of bad hombres rode into town and held up the post office which also served as the bank. In the process the postmaster was shot. The robbers got away on horseback. Within a few minutes the sheriff and a posse were mounted up, riding out after them. And they soon came back with them, their hands tied behind them. A quick trial was held, followed by a public hanging, all within a few hours of the holdup. My dad never stole anything ever. He never had any guns around the house either.

Our house in Van Nuys was built in 1918, when the town was in development. There were not many building codes in those days. In fact some of the older houses around still used an outhouse. We had a big three car garage plus barn on the back of the lot facing Haseltine. Over the door, there was a sign—GEORGE F CRUM ELECTRCAL CONTRACTOR PHONE 217-J. That was in the days when you picked up the telephone and asked the operator at the central to connect you with your desired number. The telephone central was a giant patch board with ten or fifteen girls in front of it, continuously switching patch cords around.

My dad always had an old worn out car sitting in the garage. I can remember an Essex, with slanted windshield. I used to sit in the driver's seat, running through the gears, working the steering wheel, making the engine noise with my mouth. Kids had imagination those days--no TV and just barely a radio. We made many of our own toys. Take an old roller skate, a piece of two by four, a few nails, some ingenuity, and you could have a great scooter to terrorize the sidewalks with. We decorated these scooters with bottle caps and all sorts of discarded materials.

The garage was full of tools and electrical equipment from when Dad was in the electrical business. I had access to all of it. Around the age of ten I was fooling around with electric motors, batteries, relays, telephones, all that stuff. After the chickens were gone, I made a shop of my own in the vacated chicken coop. I had an old discarded telephone wired into the house phone line. I got the greatest kick out of listening in on my sisters' conversations with their boyfriends. I also wired the door handle to a Ford ignition coil and a stoplight that I found in the local auto wreckers. When somebody opened the door, the big red stoplight came on, and simultaneously, the person holding onto the door handle got a real jolt from the Ford coil.

Eventually, I moved my bed and slept out there for several years, Snooty and me. One of my innovations was an electric operated door for Snooty which I controlled from my bed. When she wanted out in the night, I just pushed a button which turned on an electric horn motor which wound up a string which in turn lifted her door open. She went out and did her business, came back and scratched on the door until I opened it for her to come back in. It worked great. The original doggie door--electric operated. .

I must have been around five years old when my mother got a brand new wringer washing machine. It was outside of the house under a covered porch. One morning when the family was eating breakfast, the washing machine was clunking away on a load of wash, unattended. I was fascinated by those wringers, and I had to try them out. My right hand still bears the scars. I let out a scream and everybody in the house came running out. My Dad hit the pressure release handle when those wringers had me up to my wrist. He put me into the old Chandler and took me to the emergency hospital in down town Van Nuys. The attendant doctored my hand, bandaging it up to the size of a baseball mitt. I guess I was doing plenty of crying for when we left the hospital, Dad drove to the site of the Van Nuys City Hall which was in the early stages of construction. He parked the car where we could get a good view of the big steam driven pile drivers at work. It was good therapy. I must have been impressed; for years later I imitated it with a model city hall using mud bricks, steel reinforcements, etc. It was about four feet tall, with a basement and pointed top just like the real thing. And the real thing was a scaled down version of the Los Angeles City Hall which is seen occasionally on TV these days.

Walking home from school one day when I was eight years old, I felt the ground moving under my feet. I looked up and observed that these big, tall eucalyptus trees were rocking to and fro also. I did not have time to get scared before it was all over. There was no damage done within my sight. I simply continued my walk on home. But it turns out that this was the 1933 Long Beach earthquake and plenty of damage was done to our school building which was a three story brick. It did not fall down, but it was full of cracks and was declared unsafe. WHOOPY!! We got an unexpected vacation. But it did not last long, for they soon had military style tents set up as temporary class rooms. We time-shared these tents, with half day classes. This was fine except the afternoon shift in those tents was HOT. I remember a teacher by the name of Miss Allen, sweating, holding a book in her hand in front of the class, when some kid at the rear of the class, farted. Not loud but very stinky. Miss Allen was mad. She made some comments about controlling oneself.

Again, I got to watch big machinery in the construction process, except in this case it was demolition. At recess time, instead of playing baseball or marbles with the other kids, I watched a big crane with a big steel ball on the end of its cable, swing that ball full speed into the walls of the school building, over and over, knocking it down, piece by piece and wall by wall. GREAT!!

I always looked forward to summer vacations. One year, the city fathers sponsored a two-week summer camp for underprivileged boys of my age group. My mother signed me up. This camp was held in a CCC camp (Civilian Conservation Corps) out in Antelope Valley. There must have been fifty of us kids, plus a few adult camp leaders. My leader was Mr. Splain, the Van Nuys juvenile police officer. The two weeks was sort of a Boy Scout camp, where we hiked, learned to eat in a mess hall, sleep on a bunk bed, tie rope knots, etc. It was a great learning experience.

Climbing trees was great sport. I was fearless until one day I fell about fifteen feet from a pepper tree, landing on the hard ground. Somehow, I landed on my chest and the wind was knocked out of me. I couldn't breathe for several minutes. I did not give up the sport, but I was probably more careful after that.

The older kids on the block were into digging caves in their backyard or on one of the vacant lots in the area. A big hole, maybe fifteen square feet, and four or five feet deep was dug, then a roof of scrap lumber covered the hole. An entrance was made by digging a long ditch, also covered over. Inside, an Indian style fire place, complete with smoke stack out the roof was in the center of the room. Flashlights and candles were used for light. Sometimes ten or twelve kids would be in there, all sitting around the fire. One day some smart kid from another street covered the fire vent pipe. It got very smoky inside, so it was a race for the tunnel exit--the big kids first. Luckily we were not suffocated. I think that cave lasted a month or so before someone's parents got wind of it because of the dirty clothes with the knees worn through. They investigated and made us give up the cave, fill in the hole and move on to something else.

Another summer occupation those early years was visiting at my older sister's house. Her son, Donn, was only two years younger than me. So when he got to be four or five years old, my sister Mildred and brother-in-law Sam would have me down to their house for a playmate for Donn. This also gave my Mom a break. Sam worked for Standard Oil, in the oil fields on the drilling rigs. They were forever moving as oil fields were being developed. My first visit with them was in Fullerton. The next year was Anaheim. Then there was Buellton. Finally, it was Avenal, way up in the San Joaquin Valley. That was a long trip, over the treacherous Ridge Route –old highway 99. I remember making that trip in Sam's new 1935 Plymouth sedan. One episode at Avenal Donn and I were walking home from someplace. These kids, four or five of them, caught up with us and wanted to fight. Apparently Donn had heckled them in days past, so they thought this was a good time to get even. They were all much bigger than Donn, and all but one of them was bigger than me. They followed us home and halted at the back alley gate. There we stood our ground. I told them to leave Donn alone, and I would fight the one that was my size. This was my first lesson in dodging fists. This one kid let me have it with his right fist. I moved slightly to the right, so his fist grazed my left ear. I gave him back a right to the stomach, and that ended the fight. This maneuver came in very handy a couple of times in later life, once possibly even saving my life.

That same summer Sam, Sister Mildred, Donn and I were packed in that Plymouth and headed for Hume Lake in the Sierras. Sam pitched a huge tent, setting us up for a month in a great government camp ground. Across the lake was the Hume Lake Resort, run by an old German couple. Sam went back to Avenal to work, leaving the three of us to fish, swim, hike, explore--all of the good things kids like to do. There was another family camped nearby with a kid about my age. His name was Bob Burns, and he soon became the leader. He had a rowboat, which lead to our first mistake. We rowed out to the middle of the lake and decided that was a good place to go swimming. Life preservers were unheard of except for ocean steam ships. All three of us were pretty good swimmers, so we paddled around for awhile, no problem. Then Sam spotted us and hollered from shore to get back in that boat. It was easier said than done with no one in the boat to help us climb in. We finally got all three of us back in and rowed back to shore. Sam was waiting for us. He read us the riot act.

There was a great swimming area at the head of the lake near the campground. We were instructed to do our swimming there. There was a stream flowing into the lake, with a foot bridge crossing over to the resort. The bridge was about ten feet above the water level, so it made a great place to dive from. This was number two mistake! I climbed the rail on the bridge and made a perfect dive. Only one problem--the lake was not deep enough. I scraped the bottom and came up with my stomach all scratched and bleeding. I got a lecture and treatment with the iodine bottle.

There were plenty of hazards. Rattle snakes were plentiful. I learned to go the other way when I heard one of them buzzing. But Bob Burns liked to pitch rocks at them to get them good and mad. I would grab Donn and move away.

It was a great summer. The month went by fast. Sam returned to break camp and take us home to Avenal. Before we left one evening he built a big camp fire. The people in the surrounding camps gathered around the fire, and we all started singing. Four CCC boys from a nearby work project joined us with their two guitars. A great time was had by all.

Back at Avenal, it was near the summer's end and soon back to school. So it was time to go back to Van Nuys. The question was how?? No one in the family happened to be going that way. It was decided that I should ride the bus. Mildred talked to my Mom at home, so someone would meet me at the bus station in San Fernando. The next day Mildred took me and my suitcase to the Avenal Greyhound terminal and purchased a ticket for me. She had other business to take care of and the bus was not due for a few minutes. We said our goodbyes; she handed me the ticket and left. All is well. The bus came, and I climbed on. I think it took about an hour before the bus pulled into Colingo. I got on the right bus but going north instead of south. The bus driver looked at my ticket and put me on a bus going back to Avenal. There would not be another going south until the next day, so I called Mildred. She picked me up, and I stayed another couple of days. She had found a friend who was driving down and would be glad to have me along. I don't remember the ladies name, but I do remember that she had a nice big Buick AND a big colorful talking parrot. It was back to Van Nuys. Summer vacation was over, and it was back to school.

I did not have a bicycle of my own, but one day a friend came to the house on his twenty-six inch balloon tired bike. I had never ridden a bike before, but I didn't tell him that. So he agreed to let me try his bike. I climbed on from the curb and rode off like an old pro. I went clear around the block then headed home where this kid and Jeannie and Snooty were waiting. Everything was going fine until I neared that curb, and I realized I did not know how to stop or even slow down. I plowed into the curb going full speed. I went over the handlebars and tumbled onto the dirt-parking strip right at their feet. It was very embarrassing.

CHAPTER II
1935----1940

I was a busy kid but never much interested in sports. My Dad took me to a baseball game once. We watched Bob Feller pitch a no hit game. But I always seemed to have more interesting things to do. One summer my Dad got me a helper's job working in what was left of the pipe organ business. The talking movies made pipe organs obsolete for the theatres, so there were many surpluses on the market. The old organ factory on Van Nuys Boulevard was closed, so the employees turned to servicing and dealing in used organs which the theatres were getting rid of. This is where I fit in. I went with the organ mechanics to the theatre, climbed around in the organ loft pulling out electric cables, doing general "gopher" work. I was involved in a couple of installations; one I remember well was in a funeral parlor. I got a real education on coffins. Another used organ I helped install was at the Canoga Park High School Auditorium. That was a big job, which took several weeks. I spent many hours high in the organ loft with the big pipes, again mostly gopher work for the organ expert, Mr. Ferris. He was pretty old and not too fast on his feet, so I was kept busy chasing up and down stairs and ladders for tools and materials. I earned fifty cents a day for my services.

"Crum Family 1935"

When I was eleven years old my Dad bought me a balloon tired cycle for Christmas. I had a paper rack on the back, and I taught Snooty to ride on that rack. We did fine together, and she loved it. She never fell off. Those days, all American bikes had New Departure coaster brakes which were very safe. All you had to do to stop was put backward pressure on the pedals. I took mine apart several times, keeping them well cleaned and lubricated. My life became centered on that bicycle for the next few years. I went all over that San Fernando Valley on it. There was not a traffic problem then, so I could ride to Sherman Oaks, Reseda, Burbank, anyplace with no problem. My neighbor friend, Bill Pogue, and I really got around, on Saturdays or whenever school was out. During Christmas vacation one year we made little trailers to pull behind our bikes. We pulled these up into the hills, and cut holly and mistletoe; all we could carry on our bike and trailer. With this we set up shop on a Van Nuys Boulevard sidewalk and made some Christmas money.

"Jeanie Snooty Bill 1936"

Another time Bill Pogue and I rode our bikes out to the RKO movie lot in Encino. We found an opening under the fence and had a great time playing on old WW I military vehicles and the old western cow town street. I remember spending whole days out there; it was a kid's paradise. Then one day we were climbing around in the old saloon when a crew came out to use the set. It was going well until some one looked up and spotted us hanging in the rafters above. We were caught red-handed, given a good lecture and marched out to our hole in the fence. We were told not to come back, but this movie lot was getting little use (Howard Hughes had purchased it from a defunct RKO); so it was more or less deserted. Anyway we could not resist; we were back there the next Saturday. This time we found a concrete explosives storage locker open. We made the best of that find, carrying out all we could handle. This included a couple pounds of black powder, a couple dozen electric blasting caps, assorted color smoke bombs. What a find!

We hid all this good stuff under a trap door in a part of my shop. A hidden push button switch operated a solenoid lock to open the trap door. Only Bill Pogue and I knew how to open that trap door. Our first trial was with the dynamite caps. We took a few of them, along with a dry cell battery and a roll of twisted pair wire, on our bikes out to a dry wash a couple miles from home. We walked up the wash a good distance from the road. When we reached a likely spot we went about experimenting with electric dynamite caps. We dug a shallow hole in the sand, attached the wires to the cap, and then covered it up. Rolling out the wire a good distance from the burial site, we then sat down and proceeded to connect the battery. BLAM, the dirt raised up, sand scattered, and all of a sudden the nearby dry weeds were on fire. We were quite surprised, and we quickly tried to put out the fire by throwing sand on it. With no tools to scoop up the sand, it was apparent we could not stop it from spreading. We took off for our bikes and the road. We pedaled fast headed for home. We met the fire trucks when we were almost home. They were headed for the dry wash. We continued on home, never saying a word to anybody.

Another experiment was almost a disaster. I, by myself, dug a foot deep hole in the vacant lot. I poured some black powder in the hole, installed a dynamite cap with wires attached. Then I covered the powder with about a two pound rock. I backed off a little way then connected the battery. **BLAM.** That rock went sailing straight up, along with a cloud of dust. My neighbor, Lindy the cop, came running over just as the dust settled. He was excited and expected to find some sort of catastrophe, but I told him it was only a Fourth of July cherry bomb. He took my word for it and went back home.

We had fun with the smoke bombs, too. They were less dangerous even though they were the size and appearance of a stick of dynamite. We tied one each on our bikes, lit them and then took off down the street. We pedaled as fast as we could, leaving a trail of colored smoke behind. No one ever questioned what we thought we were doing or how we were making the smoke.

I had nothing but fun with this stuff, learning to respect explosives. I never did get into trouble with them. I think there was still some of it left under that floor when I left home a few years later. I have to wonder though, when reading today of all the required safety features and recalls of kids toys, how did I ever survive past kindergarten.

I moved on to Junior High School. This at that time was included in the same complex as Van Nuys High School. It was clear across town, so I rode my bike, rain or shine. The school provided a fenced in area with racks to park the bikes in. In the Wintertime, it could get wet. And with any big rain, the dry wash, which emptied into Tyrone Avenue, became a river running down through town. The city erected temporary foot bridges across at strategic locations so that pedestrians could cross.

The muddy water flowed very fast, and at times was deep. Some cars couldn't make it. Many would drive right up to the water's edge, size it up and then turn around and go back. Others would ease through, and some of those would get stuck in the middle when the engine drowned out. My buddy, Bill Pogue, and I, watched the helpless people. First, they would try in vain to restart the car, and then they would climb out on the running board and plead for help. Usually, someone would throw them a rope and tow them out. On Saturday when everybody did their grocery shopping, one of these crossings could be quite busy with lots of stalled cars. Bill and I went into the towing/rescue business. We borrowed my brother-in-law's 1927 Chevrolet, which had big twenty-seven inch wood spoke wheels. This made it high and dry, so we could ford that stream with no problem. We just parked it on one side and waited for a car to stall. Our price was five bucks, which usually included helping them restart the engine once they were towed to dry land. We made a good amount of spending money on Saturday and Sunday as long as that river held up. Again—safety wasn't considered. I don't think there was any such thing as auto insurance or life insurance for that matter. Not in my family anyway. This must have been 1936, '37 or maybe 1938. That's how things were those days, we were FREE people. There were no leash laws, no seat belt laws, no helmet laws, very few doctors, no income tax, and 3% state sales tax. All the kids knew Mac, the local beat cop, who always had a ready lecture but never a ticket. How did we youngsters ever survive without all these laws passed to protect us?

The town of Van Nuys had a farmers' atmosphere. Outside the town borders, it was mostly orchards, walnuts, citrus fruits, apricots and alfalfa for the dairies. In the wintertime, we had our smog problems, as the citrus farmers would light up their kerosene smudge pots whenever the temperature got too low. The smudge pots were scattered throughout the orchards, serving to keep frost off the fruit. The EPA people would drop dead if encountering this remedy today. The black soot from those smudge pots was so thick, when you woke in the morning you were forced to pick the black bougers from your nose.

Most of the farmers came to town to do their shopping on Saturdays, so grocery business was great, year around. At about age fourteen, I got a Saturday job sacking groceries. Then the policy was to sack, then carry them out to the car. This was at a locally owned store named Foodmart, an early version of today's supermarket. For some reason, shopping baskets had not been invented. The five dollar boxes of groceries were heavy, and sometimes the car (or truck) was a block away as the stores did not provide parking lots. I worked my butt off on Saturdays for ten cents an hour. Once in awhile one of the wealthier farmers would hand me a quarter or fifty cent tip. I could have made good use of some of our present day child labor laws.

My sister Helen had worked at the local F.W. Woolworth store for a number of years and was in good standing with the manager. In 1937 she got me a temporary Christmas season job. I remember the year well because this manager, whose name was Chris, told me that in order to work for Woolworth, I had to take out a Social Security card and number. Social Security was brand new at that time, so I had never heard of it. But I complied and was quite proud of my new status. I worked there through the Christmas season and on through the January inventory. In fact, several of my sisters were employed there that year. It was practically a family affair.

These were great years at junior high. I made new acquaintances, one of whom turned out to be a life long friend, Jack B. Clark. Also there was Jim Allison, and Tom Russell. All of the scattered grade school sixth grade classes converged at Van Nuys High seventh grade, so there were lots of new kids. And girls! I found that I was pretty well known. Each new class that I went to the teacher knew at least one of my older sisters.

Jack and I became very good friends early on, in school, after school and Saturdays. I would walk home with him after school, and in this way I became acquainted with his mom. I rode my bike over there sometimes on Saturday and became acquainted with his Dad. For some reason his folks liked me so when it came time for their vacation, they asked me to go along. It was great. We had a two week campout at Hume Lake in the Sierras. I will be forever grateful for that trip; I can still remember the full moon shining through the pine trees. I also remember a misguided fishing hike from the Hume Lake road down to the Kings River, following Ten Mile Creek. It looked from above on the road like a reasonable hike.

It wasn't too bad going down but that took several hours, so by the time we got down to the river, it was time to start back. Now this was a tough climb which took hours. Jack and I, Jack's dad and younger brother Ted, were one pooped group of fishermen, and we never got to wet a line.

Back home about this time, some of us pooled our money (ten dollars) to buy a Model T Ford. It had a wooden body, which must have been the forerunner of the station wagon--only this was open air. The only glass was the windshield. We could get about ten kids in it. The starter didn't work, so we all piled out and pushed. We took turns driving the back roads of Van Nuys. I kept it at my place in the old three car garage. It was fun for a month or so, until one day the driver took a corner too fast, running into a dirt bank with the right front wood spoke wheel. The wheel collapsed, and the car went down. We called the local junk yard to come and get it.

Another adventure with a Model T was with a kid named Russ. He had talked his Dad into buying this relic with the agreement that it would not be driven out of the yard until Russ turned sixteen and had a driver's license. Well, Russ got the T to run and the temptation was too great. One Saturday we all piled into this crate and drove to the other side of town where a kid named Merve Mcguire lived with his grandparents. The granddad had an assortment of Model T's. In fact, that's all the old man would drive. We borrowed a license plate from one of his T's, hung it on Russ's T, and took off for the old swimming hole in North Hollywood. This was an off limits sand pit on Laurel Canyon that was closed because it had filled with water. It made a great skinny dipping water hole, very private because the water was at least twenty-five feet below street level. No telling how deep the water was. Of course there was no lifeguard, in fact the area was fenced and posted NO TRESPASSING. We went there quite often in the summer time. This time it was a hot June day. We arrived about noon and parked Russ's T on Laurel Canyon under some nice shade trees which lined the road. Some of us had already climbed the fence when a black and white patrol car pulled up. They had every intention of hauling us in for trespassing, but they got side tracked with the registration and license plate of the vehicle. They radioed in and found the license number belonged to a different vehicle. Poor Russ was in for a lot of trouble. The cops left us and the car but hauled Russ to the Van Nuys Police station where they held him until his Dad came for him. That was the last he ever saw of his Model T.

I did well in junior high as I was very studious. I took all the required courses with ease. I did better in the academic shop courses. I took a different shop each semester to see which I liked better. In the end, it was solid woodshop with Jack Clark. We made furniture. We made ocean going paddle boards, toboggans, you name it--we made it. My son still has today a mahogany bookshelf that I made. Some of the other furniture I made and gave to my married sister was lost in a warehouse fire. Jack and I each made a big mahogany paddle board one year. We would load those boards on top of his '32 Chevy coupe and head for Santa Monica. Sometimes we would take our sleeping bags, spending the night on the beach. This was mostly a Wintertime sport as that's when the waves were biggest. I never did master that board. I would crest a big wave and be doing fine, but at some point the board would try to pass up the wave, nose over, and I would have to ditch to avoid being hit. It was always a bad tumble below that big breaker. There were no lifeguards around either.

About this time, my sister Helen and her husband, Bob, bought an old house almost directly across the street from my folk's house. I began spending a lot of time over there helping them fix it up. Bob was very patient. He taught me a variety of trade secrets. He always let me do things that the adults usually did which made me feel pretty big. Then too, when it came to any electrical repairs, I was able to show him a thing or two. Any way, we got along fine.

One Sunday in the winter of '39, Bob offered to take me, my new toboggan, and friends to the mountains to play in the snow. I invited Jack and his girlfriend, Peggy, Jimmy Allison and his girl (I don't remember her name), and I invited Carol Myers for myself. It was a pretty cozy carload. We all had fun. There were six of us kids and the driver, Bob, in his 1939 Chevy sedan. The day was without mishap and an early experience with girls. Actually, Carol was a first love for me, as a year or so before, I went to her house for a birthday party-- boys and girls and at night yet. I remember playing "spin the bottle." Carol managed to have it stop at me. The lights were turned out, so we had a big juicy kiss—my first. Sometime after this Sunday outing to the snow, we were gathered in the auditorium at school. I very foolishly stuck my foot out in the isle and tripped Carol as she was walking by with her girlfriend. She almost fell flat on her face. She was mad and did not speak to me for a year. And I was too stupid to apologize, so that ended our romance.

My friend Jack had been working at the Mid City drug store for about a year, after school and nights, Saturday and Sunday. Our entire group envied him for the steady job that he had, even if the pay was only twenty cents an hour. This drug store, in downtown Van Nuys, belonged to a chain of about ten stores, another of which was in Sherman Oaks. Jack put in a good word for me, and I landed the same job in this store. The only problem was getting there and back.

My mother had come into a 1934 Ford sedan from my old Uncle John who was now retired from the railroads in Kansas and was living with us. My Mom looked after him and collected his pension and Social Security. Anyway, she got a driver's license and was spouting her independence in this car for a year or so. No one in the family except old Uncle John would ride with her. In the first place, she was so short she could barely see over the steering wheel. Second, she grew up in the horse and buggy days, so she expected that V8 auto to mind as well as her horses. One day going down Victory Blvd, she scared herself into giving up driving when trying to pass another car. The car did not get much use for a year or so after that. Then I got this job in Sherman Oaks and this was a little far for the bicycle, especially at night going home. Therefore, although I was fifteen and would not have a driver's license for another year, I started driving that Ford to work. Then it worked up to taking it to school and going directly to work after school. So gradually, I took possession of that car. I bought new Kelsey-Hayes sixteen-inch wheels and tires for it. I bought a radio, and eventually I bought a Sears and Roebuck short block engine and installed it with my brother-in-laws help.

All was going well. I had myself a neat car, a steady job which would buy gasoline for it (gas was fifteen cents a gallon or seventeen cents for 100 octane). Then one Sunday, going to work down Van Nuys Blvd, I was going about fifty-five miles per hour when some old geezer in a 1936 Pontiac, let out a hitchhiker at the right hand curb, then proceeded to make a U turn right in front of me. I slammed on my brakes, the back wheels locked up so when we came together, I was going sideways down the street coincidentally when the Pontiac was right in the middle of its U turn. WHOOOMP! The fenders and running boards, end to end of both cars, were flattened back into the body. Front and rear doors were crushed. I went flying inside, forward and towards the right, gashing my head on the rear view mirror. The other driver was not hurt and stated that he had his arm out for a left hand turn (no turn signals those days). I had to dispute that because the pancake effect of the collision (his vehicle left side and my right side) would not have left much of his arm.

A passing police car stopped to see if any one was injured. They joined into the conversation about who was at fault. They looked at my skid marks and determined that I was going a little fast. They looked at the other driver's age and sided with him. Neither of us had insurance. I don't remember if they even asked to see a driver's license. I made my car go around the block to a friend's house, and then I continued on to work on foot. When I got to work, I called home to tell them the bad news. They had already heard from a friend that had passed the accident and recognized the car. The car appeared totaled. But after getting it home and giving it a close inspection, there was no damage done to the frame or running gear. The two cars had come together so flat, the damage was confined to the impact areas, body, fenders and running boards. So I looked it over, consulted some mechanic friends and decided to keep it and change out the whole body. I started prowling the junkyards and found a complete four-door body just like my original except it was painted black. I paid the junk yard thirty-five dollars for it. I don't remember how I got it home but I did. I spent the next month, mostly under that Ford, getting the old body off and the new one bolted back on. It turned out to be quite an ordeal, but I finally completed it. Then I had the left side fenders painted black to match, and I was back in business with an all black Ford in place of the tan. The whole thing cost me about fifty dollars. I was quite proud of myself.

CHAPTER III
1941-----1942

When I reached the age of sixteen, I obtained a driver's license, and was finally driving legally. My friend Jack got his license about the same time, so we planned a trip in his '32 Chevy coupe. We got my brother-in-law, Bob, to overhaul the engine. Also, we went to the junk yard and found an old twenty gallon Packard gas tank. Securing this inside the rear of the car, we spent the next month siphoning gasoline, mostly from farmer's tractors which were left sitting out overnight. We finally filled that tank.

About this time, Jack's folks traded in their '36 Nash for a '39 Pontiac four door sedan. Jack could not wait to get that car out. One Sunday, his Dad let him use it to go to the movie, double dating. Jack and his girl Peggy were in the front seat, me and my girl, Joyce Splain, the juvenile policeman's daughter, were in the back. We were zipping along on Van Nuys Blvd near Sherman Way, when somebody up ahead stopped. The street was wet from a recent rain so that heavy Pontiac slid into the car ahead. It was a mild rear-ender, not too much damage done. But Joyce, in the center of the back seat, flew forward and up, striking her head on the dome light. Her forehead was cut badly. She was bleeding all over the place. She asked for my handkerchief, but I had none. How embarrassing! A passenger in another car gave her one. A Good Samaritan offered to take her to the emergency hospital. I was asked to go along. I declined with the excuse that I had better stay with Jack and the damaged cars. Peggy went with her at my suggestion. About an hour later, Joyce and Peggy came back from emergency. Joyce had some stitches and many bandages. But she insisted she was ok so we should continue on to the movie as planned. We had a hamburger at the local drive-in. All is well, I thought.

I took Joyce home and went in with her. Her dad was away, working the night shift. Since he was a police officer, some one at the emergency had seen fit to inform him about his daughter's accident. He in turn called to tell his wife. She was waiting for us, in bed reading a book. She called for us to come into the bedroom. She wanted to talk to us. I was embarrassed to enter the lady's bedroom, but I had no choice. What a beautiful woman. There was not much of her exposed, but what there was made her daughter look sick. She first scolded Joyce for not calling her about the accident. Then came my turn—"Why did you not see Joyce to the hospital?"--and I had no answer. I did not see Joyce again for some time.

When school was out Jack and I were all prepared, sleeping bags and suitcases tied on top of his car, cook stove and groceries in the rear along with that huge gas tank. We took off before dawn one morning in June, 1941, heading north on 101, which was Ventura Blvd at the time. I remember spending the first night on a side road that led up to a hilltop. It must have been in the vicinity of Watsonville. The next morning we made it to South San Francisco and needed gas for the first time. We hunted down a service station that advertised "TRUCK RATES" and pulled in. I told the attendant that we could hold thirty gallons which qualified us for the discount. He agreed and started pumping. He soon ran the eleven gallon Chevy tank over, gave us a dirty look, and started to hang up his hose. I then opened the trunk lid to expose the twenty gallon tank, telling him "here is where the rest goes."

We drove all the way up to Oregon on 101. Someplace in Oregon, we switched to Highway 99, traveling as far north as Roseville. There we visited a druggist friend by the name of Migo or something like that. He was a great guy, in his mid-forties. We stayed there overnight, and then headed for the Oregon Caves. We made that tour, and then headed to Crater Lake. There we broke out our fishing poles, made the hike down to the lake where we rented a boat, purchased some worms and went fishing. I hooked into a big rainbow which promptly tore up my tackle and was gone. We didn't have the boat for very long, so we gave it up and made the long hike back up, empty handed. We went back to our campsite beside some hot springs where we got to wash in hot water for a change.

We left Oregon and headed back into California. One night when it was time to make camp, it was raining lightly. We ate something, and then spread our sleeping bags perpendicular to the car, with our head under the running board. In the absence of a tent, this worked fine.

We zigzagged back and forth through Northern California. I don't remember how many times we crossed the Sierras. I remember going by Lake Tahoe, then Sonora. It was almost a ghost town in those days. It was all-original. The hot weather made us very thirsty, so we decided to have a cold drink. We picked an old store, strolled up to the counter and asked what I don't remember but the counter man poured us each a beer. We didn't say a word, drank it down and strolled back out, laughing all the way back to the car. Then we headed up the highway toward Sonora pass. We stopped at Strawberry Lake where we spent a day swimming before continuing up the pass. That Chevy grunted going over that pass, as the road was (still is) long and steep. We spent the night at about the 8000 ft level after crossing the summit. We had a nice campsite courtesy of the US Forestry Service.

Next morning we continued on down out of the mountains, got on US 395 headed south to Bishop where we turned off of the highway and climbed back into the mountains again. We went as far as we could with the car (the road ended), pitched our camp, and bedded down. Next morning we got up, had breakfast and started hiking further up with the goal being Gold Lake. There, we tried our luck at fishing again, with the same rotten luck. Actually, the fish were plentiful; we were just not skilled at catching them in that clear-clear water. By the time we had our bait in the water, the fish were all scared away. I remember Jack getting disgusted and skip-throwing his five dollar pocket watch across the water after an old timer came down the trail with a whole string of nice Golden Trout. This concluded our fishing.

We continued south on 395 down to Mohave someplace I don't remember just where. I do remember we were out of groceries and money. We had shredded wheat with mustard for breakfast. Actually, we had a dollar left and after making careful calculations on our gas vs. miles home. We flipped a coin and decided to have a hamburger at lunchtime. Then we continued on home, arriving at about dark, on a Saturday evening. This had been a great two week adventure in my young life.

September found me back in school and back to work at the Mid City Drug Store. The drug store was quite an education in itself for a sixteen-year-old. I worked the late shift, after school until closing time. I learned to be in charge of the candy counter, liquor and tobacco which were all grouped together at the front of the store. I waited on drug item customers as well, but my prime responsibility was candy, liquor and tobacco; keeping the inventory and ordering for these items. I also did the janitor work which was mostly accomplished late evening hours when the customers thinned out. I mopped and waxed the floor twice a month. I washed the big display windows as needed and pasted on new sale advertisements sent out by the head office. Once in awhile I would make a delivery, usually to some movie star or VIP that Al Goodman, the manager, was catering to. Saturday nights at that tobacco and liquor counter I served many of the stars who had small ranches on out Ventura Blvd in Encino. They would stop into our store on their way to Hollywood. Since my hangout was the front of the store, I had first crack at them. Some of the lady clerks would come undone at the sight of Clark Gable. He came in several times, usually for cigarettes or candy bars. One night he came in, dressed in a tux, picked up two five cent candy bars from the counter and then handed me a dime. I told him to pick another one because they are nickel each or three for a dime (that was the going rate those days at the cut-rate drug stores). He thanked me and picked up a third.

We had a lady clerk, in her early thirties. She was married to a big fat Indian who was a real nice guy but apparently not a good mate in bed. One night Jean asked me to take her home after closing because her husband was out of town on business and she needed a ride. She was not very attractive besides being at least ten years my senior, so I didn't have the slightest notion of what she had in mind. We locked up the store, set the alarm and went around in back to my '34 Ford. We drove to her house which wasn't far, pulled up in front, and she asked me in for a drink. I was all for it, but it turned out she was serving gin. We emptied her bottle, but I still didn't catch on to what she was really after. We just talked and talked about the store and what a horney old goat Al Goodman was. About midnight, Jean suggested we run down to the corner liquor store and pick up another bottle which we did. Returning, we finished off that bottle. It was around 2 A.M. when I decided I better get going home. I made it home ok but my mother was waiting up for me. She was about to read me the riot act when I told her I had been to a birthday party with employees of the store. "Oh well, that was OK." How gullible mothers can be.

I learned about alcoholics and druggists who couldn't leave the stuff alone. Those days the prescription drugs were put together from bulk supplies by the pharmacist, as ordered by the doctor. So he had access to all the morphine and the likes. It was not even locked up. So in the almost two years that I worked there, there were quite a few pharmacists hired and fired, mostly those who worked the night shift. They would be back there behind that big window, whistling away pretending to be busy filling prescriptions, then later in the evening they would disappear into the stock room and fall asleep. Hopefully, no new business asking for the pharmacist would show up. This might go on for a few weeks, getting worse all the time. Then we would get a new pharmacist for the late shift.

Then there was Mr. Harris, the manager of the new Lorina Theatre across the street. He always wore a tux. He drank nothing but Four Roses, and he drank it by the gallon. About 7 P.M. each night after the ticket line was gone and everybody was seated inside watching the movie, Mr. Harris would pay us his first visit to pick up a half pint of his favorite, putting it into an inside coat pocket. Back across the street to the theatre and his office he would go. About 8 P.M. he would be back for his second half pint. And so, by 11 P.M. when the theatre was closing, his regular consumption was four one half pints. And he still walked. And he must have driven home. He sure kept me busy keeping up the inventory of Four Roses. I had cases of that kind and size in the stock room. At one time, Mr. Harris decided to go on the wagon. I think it lasted for about six months before he started in again. In the meantime I was stuck with all those cases of Four Roses which would be a ten year supply without Mr. Harris and his habit. I often wondered how long that man lived.

I experienced a death one Sunday at the drug store. I was going out the long hallway which led to the stockroom and the rear entrance to the store. Before I got to the stockroom door, here was a big man, in his mid fifties, lying face up on the floor. He was unconscious, I thought, so I hollered at the pharmacist for help. Somebody also called for an ambulance, but it was too late, the man was gone. We learned later that at home he wasn't feeling well and had decided to go to the drug store for an Alka-Seltzer. He made it to the store all right but only as far as inside of the back door. Lucky he didn't have his heart attack while driving to the store.

Since no one talked much about sex those days, condoms were a very hush-hush subject. In the drug store, they were kept in a special drawer all by themselves. And when a customer came in to purchase them, he always asked for a male clerk, usually the druggist. It really didn't make any difference because whenever that drawer was opened, all the clerks in the store knew what the customer was getting. Sometimes a customer would come to me for some, which was fine except there were so many different names for them. One night a regular customer, in his forties, came in and asked me for some 'merry widows.' I had never heard that name before so I proceeded to ask the lady clerk Mrs. Livingston. The customer shouted at me, "Don't ask her for Christ sake." So, I turned away from Mrs. Livingston. I got the druggist who walked directly to the special drawer, took out a package, slipped it to the customer, and rang up the one dollar. The customer, by now very embarrassed, left the store. Neither he nor his wife ever came back.

There were some other embarrassing occasions. Some of the customers who lived nearby would come in with their family. A couple of them had daughters whom I knew from school. So when it came that time of the month that there was a need for Kotex, the daughter would be conspicuously absent from her mother's side at the store. But I knew.

One Sunday, one of the movie moguls who lived nearby was in the store accompanied by his colored chauffeur. While the movie guy was back further into the store, this chauffeur cornered me and asked about my car. I told him, "Yes, I have a '34 Ford sedan out back in the parking lot." His eyes lit up and he says, "How bout driving me and a couple of friends to San Pedro tonight after work? I will buy the gas and I will have you a colored girl which will show you a real good time." I told him no thanks. He pressured me for awhile until his boss finished with his purchases and then they headed out the store together. I have often wondered since what kind of trouble I saved myself by declining this offer.

About this time, school began to take second priority relative to my drug store job. In fact, between my job, my car, and girls, my schooling was falling apart. It was 1941. I was sweet sixteen and ready to get into any sort of trouble. I am grateful that drugs were not available to kids those days. My friend Jack was involved with a steady girlfriend, so I did not see so much of him. But there were others who joined our circle. There was Bud Kissell, Ken and Wilfred Woodmansee, Ken Elson, a Japanese kid that we called Katz. There was the Mistich Brothers, Milt and Chuck. Milt, when I first knew him, worked as an usher at the Van Nuys movie theatre. I think younger brother Chuck, delivered newspapers. Their parents were immigrants from Yugoslavia. The parents collected all the money that the boys earned, kept it in the sugar bowl and doled it out as needed. They didn't speak very good English, but the mother made the greatest apple strudel.

Jimmy Allison and Katz worked in the new super market in town. Bud Kissell worked weekends with his brother-in-law moving furniture. The Woodmansee brothers, new to the area from Colorado, (we called them Oakies) worked at a dairy outside Van Nuys, milking cows. Tommy Russell drove a tractor for his girlfriend's father, plowing an orchard. Everybody had a job, and had spending money.

These were probably my greatest years: 1940, '41 and '42, when I was 15, 16, and 17. In the summer of 1940, I was pretty sweet on a girl whose name was Ruth. I had become acquainted with her in one of my classes. She was new to Van Nuys High because of some zoning problem in that she lived half way between Van Nuys and North Hollywood, so she had previously been going to North Hollywood. Anyway when the semester ended, we were sweethearts, I thought. She had a cousin, Joyce, who had come from Salt Lake City to spend the summer. Joyce was a real doll. I introduced her to Jimmy Allison. Joyce and Jim and Ruth and I had a real good summer in my '34 Ford. We spent a great deal of time at Pops Willow Lake picnicking, swimming, etc. Good fun. The next year, Ruth went back to North Hollywood High and turned me off when I went out to her house. In fact, one day I went out there with the excuse of seeing her older brother. Ruth met me at the door with some damn sailor accompanying her. I got the message that time.

In the fall semester of 1941, our group seemed headed for trouble. There was lots of partying with me supplying the beer and the booze from the drugstore. We were ditching school quite regularly, going to the beach or the desert or where ever the notion took us. One hot day, several of us hitchhiked to the beach. We split up, arranging a rendezvous in downtown Santa Monica. My half of the group arrived at the chosen street corners first and was waiting for the other half when a car pulls up in front of us. Out climbs a Santa Monica High truant officer. We couldn't convince him that he had no jurisdiction over us. He took down all our names and called them into the Van Nuys attendance office. He also told us to leave his town, no beach! For ever after, whenever any two of us were absent on the same day, we were automatically marked "truant," with no written excuses accepted. This episode put me on Mrs. Prell's black list (the head of the attendance office). She had had similar trouble with my sister Grace a couple of years before me so she was all prepared for this "Crum"

We had some other good times that could have ended in big trouble. Sometimes, I had a Sunday off, so we would load my Ford up with gas, kids and whatever, and head for the desert, usually out near Lancaster. I had a spot light on the left side, police car style. We would arrive there in the middle of the night, drive down the sheepherders trails out through the bush, hunting jack rabbits or anything that moved. Some of the kids had shotguns, some 22 rifles. I didn't have a gun, but Al Goodman, my boss at the drug store kept a 32 caliber, chrome plated pistol at the store. When I told him that I was going hunting, he offered me that pistol. Of course I accepted, bought some ammo and went hunting. When it came my turn to ride the front fender (we put a gunner on each front fender), I had a ball with that six shooter. I didn't hit any rabbits with it, but that didn't matter. I sure scattered them!

Another favorite Saturday night sport was on Mulholland Drive. It was a favorite parking area for lovers. It ran along the crest of the Santa Monica Mountains where the view at night time was spectacular. We would cover my spotlight with red cellophane, pull up behind a parked car and scare the poor couple, sometimes right out of the back seat. It was mean. One time, a guy was apparently parked with somebody else's wife, so he came out of his car holding a pistol he was prepared to shoot. That '34 Ford burned some rubber leaving that spot.

I could go on telling about some of the wild things our bunch did, but I am not too proud of some so will omit. We did plenty of beer drinking but never any drugs because they just were not around. The closest act to stealing was one weekend when we were at Big Bear Lake. We went into a restaurant and ordered up. There were about six of us. When we finished eating, we discovered no one had any money. Someone looking out the window facing the street saw Tommy Russell go by driving my car, looking for us. I think it was Bud Kissell who jumped up from the table and hollered, "Hey, there goes Tommy" and made a dash for the exit. The rest of us followed, never looking back. When we caught up with Tommy and my car down the busy street, we all climbed in and made a hasty exit from town.

One Friday night, we had the usual gang crowded into my Ford. Tommy Russell was driving while I was in the back seat. Tom was always the driver whenever there was any boozing because he did not drink. It was early evening, just after dark. We were supposed to rendezvous with Jack Clark. I don't remember what the occasion was, but we were near the High School. We turned the corner onto Vesper when up a couple of blocks we could see there had been an accident. When we pulled up to the scene, there was Jack in his '32 Chevy. There was another car nearby, lying on its side. We helped the people out through the right side window which was facing up. The car was a Model A Ford coupe, with lots of broken glass. But the kids were only well shook up. I knew both of them from school.

It was debatable who was at fault, but in any case, it ended up in court and several of us were asked to appear as witnesses for Jack which we did. I noticed when walking out of the courtroom, Mrs. Prell (the school attendance clerk) was in the audience. Jack lost the case and on the way out he called Stu, the other driver, an SOB. The fight began in earnest then. A few days later, Stu was out in front of the drug store waiting for Jack to get off work. Some how the word got around and some of Jack's friends met Stu on the sidewalk across the street from the drugstore. By the time Jack got there, there was not much fight left in Stu. But an enemy was made, and every time any of our crowd played hooky, raced cars, or whatever, the word somehow got back to the authorities. Bud Kissell came to school one Monday after working a weekend down in Hollywood, where he had run into a couple of hot women. Somehow he ended up with lipstick all over his chest. He was quite proud of this, so he did not wash it off. Instead he covered it with a T shirt, and came to school to show it off to all of us buddies. Imagine how this went over with his nicety-nice girl friend when the story got back to her via the stool pigeon. And all of us friends were on every nice girl's shit list.

Another Friday night sport, was drag racing, usually out on Balboa Avenue. This was out in the country those days. It was a brand new--two lanes of concrete. It was usually my '34 Ford against whoever had their folk's car out that night. Milt Mistich in his '36 Dodge was no match for me, nor was Jack in his Chevy. There were some strip down, souped up Model A's that could put me to shame, but I would always try. Usually I would end up with a broken cluster gear in the transmission, for speed shifting a Ford those days was tricky business. One had to "double clutch" while shifting between gears. The timing of clutching and shifting was critical. If you missed, there was a terrible crunching of gears and gone were a number of teeth out of the cluster gear.

I became quite proficient at overhauling Ford transmissions. I would limp out to Tommy Russell's place which had become the group's overhaul shop. They had a big Spanish type house with a big three-stall garage. It was empty except for Mrs. Russell's new 1941 Ford. There was a big beam across the open stalls, which was great for connecting a chain hoist and lifting the rear of the car to pull the rear axle assembly (required to get the transmission out). Ford never designed his cars for easy fixing. I do not ever remember using any safety support for the car. We would hook onto the bumper with a piece of tow chain, connect onto that with the chain hoist, lift the car off the wheels, then go about crawling under it all day long until finished, never giving a thought to an accident. There was no supervision as Tommy's dad had died a few years prior. I do remember Mrs. Russell came out one day when I was working there alone and all greased up. She asked me if I would like to come in and pray with her. I don't know if she was looking at my greasy clothes, hands and face, or the dangers of the hoisted car. I turned her down.

The Russell family was very religious, GOD BLESS THEM. They had their own brand of church, held every Saturday in their living room. It was a family affair then, usually the cousins from Fontana. Jane, the only girl, was already working in Hollywood at this time and not living at home. Each of the brothers played an instrument and Mrs. Russell or one of the aunts, played the piano. At 1 P.M. each Saturday, the boys dropped whatever they were doing, went in and participated in the service. About an hour later, they would come back out, still in their greasy or dirty clothes to resume whatever they had been doing. Mrs. Russell was the most tolerant mother that ever was. She raised the four boys single-handed; her religion was her only help. They were fine people, Tommy, Jamie, Kenny and Wally. Kenny was the maverick. He seemed to get into all kinds of trouble. And Mrs. Russell never even scolded him. She would only say, "Lord, what has got into this boy?" and go into the house to pray for him. He did some time at juvenile hall.

Along came December 7th, 1941. This was a Sunday and I was at the drug store. Somebody came in saying something about a bombing. We turned on a radio and listened. Little did we know what a change to our lives this would bring? News was scarce at first; there was nothing but confusion. All long-distance transmissions were by short wave radio. Local newscasters were as much in the dark as the general public. Anyway, an hour or so went by until the casualty figures started coming in. Then we knew it was for real. Everybody got out their world maps to learn where Pearl Harbor was located. Another hour or so went by before we see some troop movements heading south down Ventura Blvd. The Army was preparing for the West coast to be bombed and maybe even invaded.

The next day was Monday, a school day. In the late afternoon, instead of going to class, we were herded onto the football field where the big audio system was set up. They had a radio piped into the system where we listened to President Roosevelt declare war on Germany and Japan. About the time the speech was ended, a P38 flew low over the school. This was the first time anyone had seen a P38 or heard the swoosh of 300 MPH flight. It was different.

"December 8th, 1941 Headlines"

We still did not realize the significance of the war situation. But it didn't take long to start feeling it. At the drug store, there was no immediate effect on stock, but outside of our store it was a different story. Gasoline was hit first, followed by sugar, meat, tires, cigarettes, coffee. You name it; everything became scarce as the military started pigging up the available supplies. The draft had already been in effect for a couple of years, but now it was in full swing. If you were between the ages of 18 to 28, you could expect to be drafted. They set up a draft board in each community (half dozen town authorities). These people monitored the school graduating classes, as well as all prospective draftees

The 18 year old graduates went first, then right up the years to 28. If you were married and had kids, that bought you some months; but before it was all over, they were drafting everybody no matter how many dependants. The only thing that could save you was to be declared 4F, which was a severe medical problem. There were a few high priority jobs also, mostly in the aircraft factories, which the draft board was obliged to consider. But within the year, skilled manpower became scarce.

There was another sad aspect to the situation. The newspapers stirred up so much antagonism for the local Japanese that they were not safe on the streets. At my house, we had a neighborhood family who was Korean. They had to wear badges that read "I am Korean" to keep from being attacked. In my estimation, the local Japanese were rounded up and put into camps for their own protection and for the sake of law and order. No way could the police protect these people. Wartime mentality is cruel, and it is not confined to the military or the enemy (as I was to experience a couple of years later at the hands of German civilians).

In February of 1942, Jack and I got the bright idea to join the Navy. We were now of the age (seventeen) that with our parents consent, we could enlist. We cut school and drove to downtown Los Angeles to the recruiting station. After we filled out some papers, we got in the line for the physical. There were many ahead of us and some behind. The idea for most was to beat the draft board out of the pleasure of drafting you, especially if you did not like the Army. Anyway, we worked our way up to the eye exam room. I was first, Jack right behind me. I moved up to this table. The medic sitting on the other side of the table opened a large book lying in front of me, turned to a page full of colored dots and said, "Read me the number." I stared at the page where all I saw was colored dots. The medic was not paying too much attention to business. Jack came to my rescue. He whispered, "Fifty-six." I said to the medic, "Fifty-six." Then he turned to another page and said, "Read me this one." I stared at that one and still could not see anything but colored dots. Jack came to my rescue again and again as I lied my way past that page. So far, so good. This medic sent me on to another test. This one was read the chart on the wall, one eye at a time. He first covered my left eye. I proceeded to read the chart with no problem. Then he covered the right eye. I stumbled trying to read that chart with my left eye. I kept trying for a couple of minutes but finally had to give up. The medic says, "I'm sorry but you flunk with your left eye." I answered, "Yes, but I can see perfect." The sailor-medic says, "Yes, but if a seagull shits in your right eye then where will you be?" So that ended my Navy career. Jack went on through the whole physical, which took most of the day with me sitting on the bench waiting for him.

Another month went by. Jack did not follow up on the Navy enlistment. My sister Helen and her husband Bob had transferred with his building materials company, Blue Diamond Sand and Gravel, to Flagstaff, Arizona. They were home for a brief visit and asked me if I would like to go back with them to work with Bob as a mechanics helper for ONE DOLLAR an hour. I had been in the drug store for approximately a year and a half and had been raised from 15 cents to 25 cents per hour. I wasn't doing well in school, so this sounded like a welcome change. Most of my friends were enlisting in the Navy and going through boot camp at San Diego. I was doing a lot of running them back to camp on Sunday nights in my Ford.

I approached my mother with the idea. She tried to talk me out of working in Arizona on the grounds of finishing school. I don't even remember talking to my dad as he was now working twelve-hour days wiring new aircraft factories. I just did not see much of him after Pearl Harbor. He was also driving a long way to work in his old '32 Buick. Anyway, my Mom did not stand a chance. I was going with Helen and Bob. So I told my boss at the drug store that I needed a leave of absence. He did not like the idea but never the less he agreed to it. So in March of 1942, I was off to Arizona in Bobs '39 Chevy sedan. We had a carload as I recall. There were the three adults plus their two kids, Leni and Duane. It was a no stopover trip. At dawn on our second day out, we were out in the desert near Indio. We viewed Patton's tank troops out there in the sand training for North Africa. We felt sorry for them, running behind a big tank with the temperature already in the nineties.

House rentals were non-existent in the area of Flagstaff, so my sister had rented a summer cabin at the Oak Creek Canyon Resort, 20 miles south of Flagstaff, near what is now Sedona. It was a great place for a vacation, swimming pool, trout fishing stream, and lots of wild life. But it was not the greatest for a working crew. The cabin had a big screened in sleeping porch where we slept on Army cots and sleeping bags, which was ok, but there was no indoor plumbing--no toilet and no shower. We had to stop in Flagstaff at a hotel, for a 25-cent shower, on the way home from work-once- a-week! My sister did the cooking for all of us for which I paid (board and room) ten dollars a week.

The work project was for the Army, a huge ammunition dump at Winslow, which is 20 miles west of Flagstaff. The ammunition storage facilities under construction were concrete bunkers called igloos. These igloos were spread over several square miles, and each one, after the concrete set up, was covered with earth, then pine trees planted on top so that it all blended in with the surrounding terrain. This was all in preparation for a possible invasion of the West Coast by the Japanese. In the early months of 1942 they were moving very fast in the Pacific, and the U.S. did not have the means to stop them. The inland ammunition storage facility was in preparation for this if it ever came. And the Army was in a very big hurry to get this job done. The work went on around the clock, seven days a week. Any one could work unlimited overtime hours. Bob was shop foreman for one shift. He put me to work on his shift, as a mechanics helper and grease monkey. The equipment that we worked on was old, being transferred from San Fernando sand and gravel companies, Blue Diamond, Graham Brothers and Consolidated. These three companies, normally competitors, pooled their equipment to form a "Joint Ventures" to get this job done for the "war effort." It was a "cost plus ten percent" contract.

I was in my glory, making $1.10 an hour plus time and a half for all the overtime. After well over a year at fifteen cents an hour at the drug store, I was all of a sudden rich. It was much harder work. Those big sand and gravel trucks had no power steering. Some of them were so old, like the 1927 Mack Bull Dogs, they had no electric start. So when I was required to move one of them onto the grease pit, I had to hunt down a truck driver to crank it for me. Weighing in at less than 150 pounds, it was all I could do to push in the clutch pedal or turn the steering wheel. Truck drivers were big men in those days.

I learned a lot about mechanic work. I moved around that big garage doing many odd jobs. I learned to change the big ten by twenty inch tires with split rims. I learned a little about diesels, working one night with the lead mechanic. I went on emergency trips out among the new igloos. When a mixer truck broke down, all hands had to drop whatever they were doing and scramble to get that truck going before the batch set up in the mixer. The batch contained what was called "panther piss," to make it fast drying when poured into the igloo forms. If the truck for any reason didn't make it to the scheduled site, and that cement hardened in the mixer, it was goodbye truck. Most of the mixer trucks were new Ford V8s, so they did not give too much trouble, but they still had flat tires now and then.

The mechanics in the shop grew tired of me borrowing their tools all the time, so one day Bob called me aside and asked me to get my own. The next day I obtained a Sears catalog and ordered a $100 set of Craftsman tools, complete with tool chest. Bob helped me pick them out. When they arrived, a week later, I spent an hour marking each one with four notches to identify them as mine, for there were many sets of identical Craftsman tools in that shop. I was very proud to have my own tool set.

I wrote my friend Jack about all the money I was earning. He wrote back that when school was out, he would like to quit the drug store and come over. I checked it out with Bob and Helen--they knew Jack very well--so they said "why not?" There was plenty of room in that sleeping porch. When June rolled around, Jack came over in his '32 Chevy. Bob got him a job running the gas pumps which were located out in front of the big shop. He was kept pretty busy pumping gas to all those big trucks. He got the same $1.10 an hour as I did. The only problem was we did not always work the same shift so Jack had to drive alone to work and back. One morning, on his way back to the cabin after a graveyard shift, he went to sleep coming down the winding canyon road, ran off the pavement and hit a post which was serving as a guard rail. That woke him up in time to steer back onto the pavement, saving him from a 50-foot fall into the river below.

Word got around back home about the money to be made out there in Arizona. Shortly after Jack arrived, here came two other sisters with their husbands. This was Betty and Ed Marks, Grace and Fred Place. Bob found a place for them in the shop also except again, on different shifts. So now, the sleeping porch began to fill. But we were working different shifts so sleeping was in shifts also. This was a busy place, somebody eating, sleeping and leaving for work at all hours of the day and night. My sisters were kept busy cooking, however, they took turns and all got along well.

One evening, Fred was filling the gasoline lanterns just outside the door—the ONLY door. It had just turned dark. Jack and I had gone to bed inside the screened porch. Fred swears he was not smoking at the time and no one called him a liar, but somehow the one gallon can of gas that he was holding became ignited. He dropped it and it spilled down the hill alongside the screen porch which was on stilts. Jack and I woke up to see flames way above the upper section of screen. It was a potentially dangerous situation, especially with the only exit being at the source of the flames. There was much shouting and scrambling towards that exit. However, the ground outside was wet from a recent shower, and the flames were just far enough from the wood cabin, that it was not ignited. The gasoline burned itself out before any real damage was done other than some lost sleep.

On the 4th of July, all of the Indians of the area moved into the Flagstaff City Park for their annual POW-WOW. They put on quite a show with lots of feathered costumes and dancing. It was very interesting. I was very impressed by the mothers sitting around nursing their infants!

Working so many hours and so occupied with our surroundings, the summer went by very fast. When September came Jack wanted to go back to school. He talked me into going back with him. We packed our belongings into his '32 Chevy, checked out at the truck shop, collected our paychecks, said goodbye to everyone, and headed down the road. On the way home, we stopped off to see the Grand Canyon. Other than that, we just drove endlessly down old Route 66. I do remember passing through Las Vegas. I think it took about sixty seconds. In 1942 it was the typical desert hick town consisting of gas station, post office and grocery store, plus maybe a bordello or two.

We made it back to Van Nuys and back to school for the Winter semester. This was Jack's last and should have been mine also, but I soon learned that because of leaving early the prior semester (and some other problems with teachers), I would come up short of credits to graduate the following spring. So I was not too happy with school again. Besides, there was all that big money to be made out there. I went back out to the drugstore one day and told Al Goodman that I couldn't work for twenty-five cents an hour again. He understood.

I fired up the old '34 Ford, buying a new set of tires for which I proudly paid cash. I looked up some of my old friends. I don't remember what the occasion was, but I was driving down Lankershim Blvd. I pulled up to a four way stop sign, intending to stop, but the other cars were in the process of accelerating. So I put that Ford into 2nd gear and accelerated with them. That was a mistake because out of the corner of my eye I see this big motorcycle cop on this big Harley starting to crank up. I knew who he was going after. I think to myself, it will take a few strokes to get that Harley going. He is on the other side of the street, so he has to get across two lanes of traffic to get on my tail. So instead of slowing down like I should have, I floored that Ford, came to a cross street and made a left crossing two lanes of traffic and zoomed down the street. That was the longest street in the world with no cross streets to turn off onto. By the time I neared the end of that street, I looked in my rear view mirror and here comes that Harley, with the red light on. I pulled over to the curb, shut down and waited. The big cop pulled up behind me, shut down the Harley and the red light, and then strolled up to my door. He was pissed! He read me the riot act. When I didn't give him any argument or back talk, he gradually calmed down. However, he said for me to proceed to the Van Nuys police station. He would follow behind, and he "would shoot my tires off if I tried any more of that runaway stuff." I drove my best to the police station, pulling away from each stop sign very slowly to avoid making any excess roar with my Hollywood mufflers. When we arrived at the station, the cop walked up from behind where he had parked the Harley and he said, "That's a nice sounding set of mufflers you have on that Ford."

He led us inside, past all of the jail cells, and into a room where he called in another cop. The two of them proceeded to lecture. At that period in time, they could not issue tickets to juveniles. However, they could lift my driver's license, which they had decided to do. I gave them a song and dance about just returning from Arizona. I was only home temporarily to get my car and return there. So I really needed that license. OK, they said, we will give you two weeks, and then you must mail it to us. We will hold it for three months. That's the way it went. I did not return to Arizona, but I did mail in my license and parked the Ford.

By now, many of my friends had enlisted in the Navy. Also, Bud Kissell, the Woodmansee Brothers, and Ken Elson, had gone to Arizona to look me up and get in on some of the big money. I was already home in California when they arrived in Flagstaff, but they did connect with Bob, who sent them someplace for truck driving jobs. In the meantime at home, I was chumming around with Milt

Mistich, who had graduated already. Milt had purchased a tractor with plowing arrangements, an old '29 flat bed Chevy and trailer to move the equipment with. He had been plowing orchards on contract for about a year and was ahead of the game money-wise. He had bought a '39 Mercury convertible which was quite an attraction to the girls. Milt had a way with the girls anyway, with or without the convertible. But it helped no doubt about that. One September night we were out together when we met a girl that he had heard about. This girl, Norma Jean, liked to do for all the boys. So we took her to a movie or whatever, then headed for the hills with her in the middle, Milt driving and me on the right. I started pawing her but being a real amateur, I got nowhere. Milt saw what's going on, so he drove me home. I said good night and went in to bed.

The next day Milt came over. He told me all that I missed out on. So a few days later, I fired up my Ford, called up Norma Jean and made a date for that night. I went to her house where I learned that she lived with her stepmother, her aunt or maybe it was foster parents. Anyway, there was no one home except Norma Jean. Something was not right for she was only sixteen or seventeen years old and always home alone at night. Anyway, we went up to Mulhulland Drive. This was my first real experience with a girl who knew what she was doing. I took her home after midnight. There apparently was still no one home.

A couple of days later, I called her again for a date. She said sure, but when the time came, I chickened out and did not show up. I had car trouble or something. Anyhow, I forgot to call to cancel. A few more days went by. Milt and I were sitting in his convertible near the school when Norma Jean came walking by with some of her girlfriends. She came over to the car and shouted, "I hate you!" I shrunk down in the seat. Milt started the car and drove off. Norma Jean, a few years later, turned out to be Marilyn Monroe-- the only girl in my life that I ever stood up.

Sometime in the fall of that year, 1942, my best friend Jack Clark, joined the Navy. His mother gave him a going away party at their house. There must have been ten or fifteen couples in attendance. I took Joyce Splaine again. She was the daughter of the local juvenile police officer. I remembered him from earlier years, but he did not remember me. Actually, he was a great friend to most of the kids, was well known and well respected. Joyce was a nice girl, with a fine personality. I had dated her several times in the past.

My mother muscled her way into this party, somehow, unbeknownst to me. I arrived at the party somewhat inebriated, and there was my mother. I somehow kept a straight face until Mrs. Clark could get mom off into the kitchen. Then Mr. Clark (we called him JH) and Jack hustled me out into the night, poured some tomato juice down me and started walking me up and down the little country road. There was a very bright moon out and for whatever reason; I started singing "Moonlight Becomes You." I blamed the whole problem on Jacks going away to the Navy. I was pretty unhappy about that. Eventually, the three of us went back into the house and joined the others at dancing, playing games and whatever. Actually, I don't remember too much else. I am sure they did not let me take Joyce home, or my mother, for that matter. I do remember Mom the next day, expressing her disappointment that I did not introduce my girl to her. I apologized, making up some stupid reason. I was pleased that she got through the night without finding me out.

I could not get too interested in school. In fact I was very restless, giving the teachers a bad time. One afternoon in October, my friend Milt said some of his friends had gone to work in Northern California on the Shasta Dam project and were making big money. He suggested that we split expenses, take his Mercury and check it out. I was all for it.

My Dad had gone to work in the shipyards in Seattle. My mother, my sister Georgia, and Sister Jeannie were living at home. Georgia had graduated from school and was working at an aircraft plant at the Van Nuys Metropolitan airport. I approached my Mother about leaving school and going to Shasta with Milt. She, of course, disapproved of me leaving school again, but I convinced her it was the thing to do. A couple of days later, Milt and I were packed into his Mercury. We drove all day long, stopping only for gas. We reached our destination late that night. Milt had all the directions from his friend. I must have slept for the last couple of hours of the trip for I only remember arriving at this place out in the woods. It was raining, dark and very uninviting. There was nobody around as it was way after working hours. We spent the rest of the night trying to sleep in that cold convertible.

Next morning, we found Milt's friend. He told us where to apply for work. We drove down this gravel road to what was called Pit Number five. It was a construction company, Heinz and Bishop, building a power house, complete with pennstock from back up the mountain with the intake on the Pit River. There were several temporary buildings gathered in the narrow Pit River Canyon. There were three or four bunkhouses, a mess hall, and the crusher producing sand and gravel for the concrete. We were directed to find a Mr. Foreman, at the crusher scale. He was in charge of the fleet of dump trucks that were by now lined up awaiting their turn to load under the crusher-hopper.

We located Eric Foreman. He was a tall slim man, with thin face and square jaw, looking the part of a foreman. We introduced ourselves and explained that we were looking for a job. After he looked us over, he asked our experience as truck drivers. Milt told him that he had more time on a tractor but that he had driven light trucks. I told him my experience in the Arizona shop as grease monkey which only occasionally required driving. Eric Forman thought it over, and then said he would not hire us, as he did not want any young Southern California "prune-pickers" tearing up his trucks. He was about to walk away when I spoke up and said, "Well, I guess you don't need truck drivers very bad, huh?" That lit his fuse! I thought maybe he would explode. He said, "I need drivers in the worst way. You two be back here tomorrow morning, 7A.M. I will put you in a truck and check you out. If you pass, you are hired." He walked off.

The next morning we were there at seven. The fleet of trucks consisted of eight Fords, and two Internationals, all of which were 4 yard dumps. These were used to haul sand or gravel from the crusher at the Pit River, to the top of the mountain where the pen stock was under construction. There were two other trucks, ancient 1924 Auto Cars 6 yard dumps. These were used to haul big rock being drag lined out of the river bed, up a steep quarter mile ramp to the top of the crusher. Eric put Milt into one of the Fords going up the mountain. He put me in one of the Auto Cars. He gave me some instruction as follows: "There are no brakes to speak of on these rigs, so you take it easy and don't get over 5 mph. You take your turn, at the drag line, back under and wait for the drag line operator to signal you to go. Proceed to the bottom of the ramp, STOP and change gears down to first. Then proceed up the ramp. Do not attempt to shift down while climbing that ramp because if that load of rock gets away from you, there is no stopping you until you go into the river." So I walked out to the truck that Erik pointed at, climbed up and started the engine. I backed into position aside the drag line, waiting for them to fill up the big bed. The steel bed extended over the cab to protect the driver from being hit by the bucket or rocks. But there was no protection from the noise. When the crusher was in operation, the noise from it was deafening. Add to that, a bucket full of boulders being dumped into the steel bed, and it was enough to wake the dead. I soon learned to exit the cab while it was being filled.

Milt and I did all right that first day. We had a job. Eric, at the end of the day told us our employer was Heinz and Bishop of San Francisco. The project consisted of five power generators with associated pen stock, spread out about twenty miles along the Pit River, one above the other. The whole thing was part of the Shasta Dam Project, and the U.S. was in a hurry to get the power going because it was needed in the ship yards and aircraft plants.

We were at Pit # 5, where the crusher, truck garage and truck scales were central to the operation. In addition, there was a mess hall complete with steel ringer for announcing chow time. On the side of the hill, was the bunk house—Army style. Room and board was ten bucks a week. It was good living. Four bunks to a room.

Milt and I had to separate. I was put in a room with the drag line oiler. He was an old logger, pretty rough and didn't smell too good either. But there wasn't much time for socializing anyway. We worked an eight hour day most of the time, plus the meal time. Mostly everybody went to bed quite early. Some of these old lumberjacks could snore up a storm.

I soon ended up working the night shift. Driving up and down that ramp got pretty monotonous. I soon gave up stopping at the bottom of the ramp to down shift. There was no challenge to that. So I would get up some speed, turn the corner onto the ramp and get about a quarter of the way up before bogging down. Then I would double clutch, shift down and continue to the top. One night, I was going through the gears very smooth, but when I let out the clutch, there was the sound of a canon. An axle had snapped. This loaded vehicle started back down that ramp immediately. I pulled hard on the parking brake before it gained momentum. It worked. I jumped out and put the biggest rock that I could carry behind the rear wheel. Then I walked down the ramp and back to the crusher to report. After that, I did just as Eric had instructed, stopping at the bottom of the ramp to change gears.

Milt and I got acquainted with a couple of teenage clowns from Weaverville, a small town to the west of Redding. They were very familiar with all of the night spots in Redding. We spent a couple of weekends prowling the night spots with them. They were heavy drinkers. They took us to the village of Big Bend, where Mt. Shasta beer was sold in one gallon wine jugs. It was very good beer; a couple of gallon jugs was just right for a Sunday afternoon.

When November came, it was Milt's eighteenth birthday, which meant that he had to register for the draft. Since he preferred to register with the Van Nuys draft board, he quit the Shasta job and left for home. I decided to stay put. I was getting along with Mr. Foreman by now. He seemed to like my work. I was driving the long trip up the mountain on the night shift with no problems. In fact, the truck mechanic had recently quit, and I was gradually working my way into that job. I told Eric of my grease monkey experience at Flagstaff. Since this job mostly consisted of greasing and light maintenance, I thought I could handle the job. He agreed to that and said until I could get into the mechanics union, he would make up the pay difference in overtime hours. That was great with me.

I telephoned my mother the next day, asking her to lock up my new tool box and put it on a Greyhound bus to Redding. About a week later, I hitched a ride on a company truck and picked up my tools. Now I really had it made. I was my own boss in this crude, open air, maintenance shop which was right on the river bank, facing the crusher. Very good pay $1.37 an hour I think it was, whereas driver's scale was $1.05. There was only one problem, the Union. Eric said I had to get down to Redding and enlist in the Mechanics Union at my first opportunity. But don't rush.

Around the second week in November, I went down to the Redding Union office. I went in, told them my story, had my wallet out ready to pay my dues, when some official sitting behind a big desk, spoke up and said NO. They had a couple of members who were out of work, and they had first crack at that job. I walked out of the building quite perplexed.

Back at the shop, I told Eric what had happened. He said to continue on as per our original agreement, but when somebody showed up from the Union, that I was to lay low so as to avoid trouble for him. So, a few more days went by and here comes this old geezer lugging his toolbox up the hill to the shop. I exited as inconspicuously as I could. Eric put me back driving up the hill, stating that there was nothing he could do since the Union was all-powerful at this job. Many of the crusher people and dragline operators were Union and the construction schedule did not allow for any trouble with them. So, that was the end of my fat mechanics job—for a couple of weeks.

I was working day shift, driving the International up the hill. It had just been in the shop for lube and oil change. I was coming down the hill, on my way back for another load when I glanced at the instrument panel, noticing the oil pressure gauge was reading zero. I pulled to the side of the road, shut down the engine, got out and opened the hood. I pulled the dip stick to find NO OIL showing. It was late in the day. All the other drivers had made their last load, so there was no chance of hitching a ride in. Since it was all down hill back to the plant, I decided I could coast back without the engine. So that's what I did. There was a little grade out in front of the plant, so I kept up my speed until the very end, rolling to a stop in front of the garage. Eric happened to be standing in the garage talking to the new mechanic. I climbed out of the cab and reported to the two of them that there was no oil pressure showing on the gauge. The two of them opened the hood and checked the dip stick. As I had found, there was no oil showing. Eric then bent over and looked underneath, checking the oil drain plug. It was gone. Obviously, it had not been tightened after the oil change. The plug and new oil were dumped on the road somewhere near the top of the hill. Eric was fuming, but he did not say too much, just walked away, leaving the new mechanic mumbling something to himself.

The next day when I showed up for work, I was assigned to another truck. I noticed the International was parked near the shop with the hood up. In fact it sat there for several days. I finally asked Eric what was happening with it. He told me they had ordered a new set of rod bearings for it. Since most truck parts of all makes and models were going to the military, there was a problem finding new parts even with the Shasta priority. I told him I was surprised that they were being replaced because I had shut the engine down before it was making any noise so there could not have been too much damage. Eric replied that he appreciated that, but the mechanic had decided to pull the pan off and replace the bearings.

After a week went by, I noticed the truck was moved into the garage and was being worked on. Another couple of days passed, and then it was back out in the parking area with the hood up but not being worked on. In fact, no one was in the garage working on anything. The first time that I encountered Eric, I asked what was happening to my truck. He scowled and said, "I fired the G.D. asshole mechanic." He went on to tell me that this guy the Union had sent, was not a mechanic at all, but he was a welder which entitled him to belong to the same local. He thought he could handle the job maintaining this small fleet of trucks because he had worked on some Model T's and A's in years past. So when it came to replacing the new hard-to-get rod insert bearings, he thought that they fit too loose, so he filed the ends to make them fit tighter. When he told Eric what he had done, that's when Eric exploded and told the guy to pack up his tools and get out NOW.

This was a big lesson in unionism. I never had much use for them. In fact, in later years I grew to hate the word. But that is another story. In this case, Eric did the maintenance work himself. I occasionally helped, and he used my tools. He offered to buy them from me but I declined.

The plant shut down for the four days of Thanksgiving weekend. The camp was nearly deserted. I was asked by one of the younger drivers whose home was in Oregon, to accompany him in his '36 Ford to see some friends up near Dunsmuir. We left early in the morning, drove down to Redding, then north up 99. We crossed the new bridge spanning the future Lake Shasta. It was a long way down to the bottom and the Pit River. That was the high light of the day. We went on up 99, turned off and drove several miles to the west to find the old farmhouse of his friends, way out in the woods. We spent a few hours visiting, then got back in the car and back to Pit # 5, arriving there in the middle of the night.

December came around bringing with it Christmas. It had been raining most of the month. As Christmas neared, the rain turned to snow. I was a long way from home with no transportation, so I decided I would remain in the camp over the holidays. The plant was to be shut down until after New Years. I informed Eric of my decision. He came back with an offer to pay me through the period if I would check on the trucks now and then, to make sure they did not freeze and so on. I told him that would be great. I dropped my mother a post card, explaining that I would not be home for the holidays.

The end of the week came, and the camp started emptying out. All the work crews were going home except for the cook and a few camp maintenance men. It was snowing hard. Somebody was playing the new Bing Crosby record, "White Christmas." I was already lonely. I wasn't even into my first day yet. One of the drivers was having trouble getting his car out of the parking lot, slipping and sliding in the snow. I went over to help him as he was one of the last to leave. After we got the car unstuck, he was about to drive out when he mentioned he was going to Sacramento. That did it. That was almost half-way home. I asked him to wait a minute while I picked up my toothbrush and a few clothes which I did and we were off.

It was a tough trip out, mostly uphill and snowing hard. We caught up with the rest of the crowd on the two lane, winding road. It was late afternoon, turning dark by the time we reached highway 299. When we headed west toward Redding, it was really beginning to look like a "White Christmas." We reached Sacramento around midnight. I had my friend drop me off in the industrial truck yard section of town where I figured I could catch a ride on a freight liner. The idea was great except that it was the Friday Night before a holiday so there were no trucks moving. I stood on the highway for an hour or so, very miserable, tired and cold. I gave it up, making for the Greyhound bus terminal. I was home the next day. I was always happy that I made it home that Christmas of 1942, because it would turn out to be my last to be with my family for a few years.

I was home that week. The plant up north would not resume operation until after New Years. We did not have the usual big family gathering, for there were too many missing. Two brothers-in-law were now in the Navy. Dad was working in the shipyards in Seattle. My great Uncle John had passed away. When I called up my friend Milt, it turned out he had been drafted into the Army, sent to Fort Lewis in Washington, discharged and classified 4 F because of asthma. So we double dated a couple of times. I took out the policeman's daughter, Joyce. She was great and apparently her folks had forgiven me for the accident episode. When it was time for me to return to work up north, I decided to take the train, San Fernando to Redding. So Milt, his girlfriend, Joyce and I spent the afternoon together, then they delivered me to the train in San Fernando.

I arrived in Redding a couple of days after New Years, hitched a ride out to Pit # 5 and reported in to work the next morning. Eric was not too happy to see me. It turned out that he had to leave his family in Redding to go up and check on the trucks. He put me back on the night shift, spreading gravel on the mountain road

CHAPTER IV
1943---EIGHTEEN

I continued with the truck driving job through January and the first two weeks in February. Then I informed Erik that, now that I would be eighteen soon, I had to be concerned with the Van Nuys Draft Board and I was quitting at the end of that week. He did not object but half heartedly said that he could get me a deferment if I were to stay on this job. I turned him down and at the end of the week, collected my pay check, gathered my tools and left for home.

I do not remember registering for the draft. What I remember was becoming very bored waiting for them to call me. All my friends were in the service by now. Everything in civilian life was rationed. I had sold my '34 Ford to my friend Tommy Russell, so I was without wheels. I decided to get a job to pass the time. I saw a help wanted sign at the local Chevrolet dealer on Van Nuys Blvd. Talking to the Service Manager, I found that they were very hard up for help. I was hired on the spot. The pay was minimum $ 40 per week, plus a fixed rate for each job completed over the minimum.

I was given an area which included a bench and locker for my tools. I was next to the only mechanic that they had left--that was because he was way beyond draft age. But he knew his business, so he always doubled the minimum rate. Me, I never exceeded it. I was given the odd ball jobs, on odd makes of cars. I really stumbled around. New cars were out of production. General Motors was building tanks and Allison engines for P38 fighters. Ford was turning out B24 bombers (over 8000 by wars end). Chrysler was making tanks, trucks, and jeeps.

Many old junkers were put back into use. I first got into trouble with an old Chevy that had a lever spring that pushed against the steering tie rod. It was for the purpose of minimizing front wheel shimmy. I had to get that tie rod out of the way to get the pan off the engine. I had the car all jacked up and was underneath on my creeper. I had undone the tie rod at one end and was not paying any attention to that powerful spring. I pried the tie rod off of the connecting ball. When it came off, it came swinging with the force of a baseball bat with my face right in its path. It caught me over the right eye. I still bear the scar. .

In the middle of May, I finally received the "Greetings, you are ordered to appear" notice from the draft board. The notice included a street car ticket to the induction center in downtown Los Angeles. I was to report on June 8th, 1943. I still had a couple of weeks of freedom, so I was determined to make the most of it.

I remember raising hell at a couple of parties. My sister Helen gave me a going away party at her new home in North Hollywood. It was a good party but most of my friends were missing, already in the service, Army or Navy. Tommy Russell was there, I can remember him doing somersaults on the hardwood floors.

On June the 8th, 1943 I was up early. After my mother fixed me a nice breakfast, I gave her a big hug and went out the door. I walked the four blocks to Van Nuys Blvd. There the electric street car waited to take me to down town Los Angeles. I climbed aboard and sat down. There were very few other passengers. In fact, there was hardly anyone out on the street. There certainly was no one there to see me off. I did not expect a band playing, but I was disappointed that at least a draft board member wasn't there to make sure that I showed up.

Thus began my military career. It was the middle of the war for the U.S. time-wise. There had not been too many victories for our side as yet. I had no idea what to expect. But I would learn fast. The first stop was the induction center in downtown L.A. It was crowded, long lines of inductees waiting for this or that. The main function was the physical. Based on my experience with the Navy physical the year before, I half expected to flunk out. But things had changed in that year. I went through the eye test with no problem, for they did not even have a color blindness test. This place was so hungry for bodies; they passed everybody that could walk.

Following the physical, I came to a desk where I was asked, "Navy or Army?" I answered Navy. I got Army. That afternoon, about fifty of us were stuffed on a bus then driven to Camp Hahn, near Riverside. They called this a reception center and that it was. We were no sooner off the bus when we were lined up and introduced to our Sergeant in charge. He wasted no time in letting us know that he was "NOT YOUR MOTHER." We were marched, single file everywhere: first, to an open air barracks, where we were assigned a bunk with blankets and given a demonstration in how the bed was to be made each morning. Next stop was the quartermaster building where we filed through and a uniform, underwear, socks, shoes, all were passed to us by a clerk standing behind a counter who took one glance and decided what size each individual required; last to the barracks and into the new clothes. Good bye civvies for the duration of the war. Wearing civilian clothes from now on would be an act of desertion.

So it went. That first week was very busy. Haircuts were high on the list. At this period in time, the media had been exploiting what had been termed "Zoot-Suiter" wars on the streets of San Pedro, mostly between sailors and longhaired Mexicans. Some of these Mexicans ended up in this Army depot where they were given a hard time at every opportunity. For example, they were the first to get their heads shaved by the barber. Some almost cried while the rest of us stood by waiting our turn and laughing at them.

We took all kinds of aptitude tests, intelligence tests, reading tests, and a blood test. Each man was issued dog tags and given an Army serial number. We learned the basics of marching. We learned the Army way of eating in the mess hall. We were told how to shine our shoes. It was a very busy week. When Sunday came around, we were allowed visitors. My mother got somebody to bring her out. It was sort of like a prison visit. We were not allowed to leave, only visiting in the designated area. My civilian clothes were packaged for Mom to take home. We met with an old family friend that my mother had contacted. A clerk in the establishment, he told us that he had sneaked a look at my test results--my IQ was 143. I had never heard of an IQ, so it meant nothing to me. I kissed dear old Mom goodbye when visiting hours were up. She left with her friend while I went back to the barracks.

The next day we were told that if our name was called, we would be shipping out. Many of us in the barracks were called. We stuffed our newly issued clothing into duffel bags, lined up in front of the barracks, marched off to a waiting train, and sent off to nobody knows where. Watching out the window, I could tell we were going east.

I became friends with a fellow a couple of years my senior. His name was Don. He was from Fullerton where his father ran a Chevrolet dealership. We were to become fast friends over the next few months. We sat and talked much of the night as we journeyed to wherever.

The destination turned out to be Army Air Corps Basic Training Camp at Kearns, Utah, on the hot plains just outside of Salt Lake City. I was grateful that I was in the Air Corps. For one thing, it was a much better assortment of people than back at the reception center. It was apparent that the better educated were sent to the Air Corps while the Zoot Suiter crowd was sent to the ground forces where they would probably land in the front lines very soon.

The barracks were open air, temporary structures. In fact, all of the buildings within the perimeter looked very temporary. They had obviously been thrown up in a hurry. The buildings consisted of barracks, latrines adjacent to the barracks, mess hall 500 yards down the road. Then there was a headquarters building. It was a busy time, six weeks of it. Rise in the morning at dawn, fall out to formation, march to the mess hall, wait out the chow line which moved very fast for it was highly organized. The chow was nothing to brag about, but it was obviously a good balanced diet. After breakfast it was drill, and drill and drill. I can still hear our drill instructor – hut two three—hut. RIIIGHT TURN- MARCH hut two three. On and on in the hot sun. After lunch, it was two hours of calisthenics and then more drilling. Then it was the obstacle course—crawling on your belly, climbing a six ft. wall, climbing a rope. Rifle range, bivouac, guard duty. We learned all the basics of being a soldier. And it was rigorous. There were no overweight persons in this training for it was tough. Following the evening chow, it was back to the barracks; draw a clean towel, out to the latrine where the showers were. After the shower, I was always ready to collapse. It was lights out at 10 P.M. A few weeks of this and I was in great physical condition, as was everyone else in my barracks. There were no drop outs.

The above routine was five days a week. On Saturday morning after chow, it was scrub down the barracks and latrine. Shine shoes; straighten out your footlocker for inspection. After inspection, it was dress for parade and weekend pass. The parade consisted of all the rookies, formed into their respective squads and groups standing at attention while the camp commander walked up and down the lines checking uniforms, rifles, etc. If all went well, the whole camp was off for the weekend, Saturday noon until Sunday evening. Following the parade, we were free to catch the bus for town.

My friend Don and I went to town (Salt Lake City) together. We soon met a couple of girls who were cousins. The one girl was the daughter of the manager of the local JC Penney store. They had the use of their father's 1941 Chrysler. We double dated most every weekend with these two girls in their Chrysler. We went to dances, picnics and wherever the gasoline supply would take us. We had lots of good clean fun with these two good Mormon girls.

One weekend I was on my own for whatever reason. I had put in my five bucks to share a community suite in the local hotel with a group of comrades from my barracks. This was a common practice of this group, each weekend, to rent one big hotel room, sharing the bill, the couches, the carpet, and the beds. I had a date with a different girl this particular week. About all I remember of it was some heavy smooching on the lawn of the state Capitol. After I told this girl goodnight, I started for the hotel. I found the hotel ok, but I had neglected to get the name of the person registering for the room. And of course, I had no way of getting the room number. To make a long story short, I had no place to sleep. The streets were deserted at this time of night, as Salt Lake City was and is not known for its night life. I wandered around for awhile, finally stretching out on a park bench and trying to sleep. It was a very miserable night.

There were many learning experiences at Basic Training; a few of them were not pleasant. KP was one of them. Each barracks took their turn in the kitchen, which was one day every other week. That day it was up at 4 A.M., march to the kitchen and try to be assigned to the easiest jobs. The dirty work came following each meal.

The meals were served cafeteria style, on metal trays. Each meal, morning, noon and night, served around 200 GIs. The tray was first scraped clean of any leftovers by the user; then it was passed along with the silverware to a KP person who dunked it into a GI can filled with detergent. A brush was run over it with the soapy water; then it was placed on a conveyer belt, which ran it through a steam wash. After the meal was over, and all the plates were washed, it was wet mop the whole area. Everything was scrubbed three times a day. This was the KP routine, 4 A.M. until about 7 P.M. Then back to the barracks to pass out.

Another unpleasant job was a turn at guard duty. We all had to take a turn at that. Four hours in the middle of a very black night out on a perimeter gate with a loaded rifle with specific orders to shoot anyone who could not identify themselves. The "WHO GOES THERE" routine, and if the password was not returned, we were instructed to shoot. And, of course, some time during your watch, some 2nd Lt. would be out to try you on to make sure you were not sleeping on the job. It was all part of the training, as there was not anything other than coyotes out there.

Everybody in the Army was paid once a month. This was a very memorable occasion the first time at Kearns, Utah. On a hot summer day, we were told to strip naked but wear a raincoat and shoes. Line up in front of the barracks and march to headquarters. Form a single line at the front door of headquarters and enter when your turn comes. Imagine standing in line in the hot sun wearing a black rubber raincoat. Fortunately, the line moved pretty fast. After entering, I observed what was going on. The first person encountered once inside the door, was a medic of some sort. He commands, "Open your raincoat and skin it back." He is looking for any signs of VD. Next stop is an officer's desk with a pile of cash. Some assistant calls out your name. You state your ASN (Army serial number). If it matches his roster, then the officer counts out your pay. You pick it up and file out the back door, down the steps. At the foot of the steps, on the ground, is a crap game with a dozen excited players, all talking to those dice. Some arrived back to the barracks flat broke.

So it went for six weeks. Upon satisfactory completion, we were elevated in rank to PFC (private first class). Each man was given a choice of three tech schools: Radio, Aircraft Mechanics, or Aircraft Armament. I felt that with my experience, the mechanics school was a sure bet. So that was my first choice. Second choice should have been radio, but I was so sure I would get the mechanics school, I put down Armament with Radio being third. I got Armament. A couple of days later about fifty out of our class boarded a train headed east again. So I was separated from my buddy Don, as he was assigned to Radio school.

Our destination this time turned out to be Lowery Field at Denver. The train trip was great. We were traveling through the night, so we were in Pullman cars, each man with his own bunk. It was high-class travel, just like in the movies. I spent much of my time standing on the rear platform, watching the scenery go by. The route was through the Rockies and the Colorado Gorge, a very popular trip in the days before air travel. I felt like a big shot traveling around the country in a Pullman, with colored porters and eating in the dining car. This Army life is looking good, even if the pay is only $52 a month.

Arriving at Lowery, our whole group from Basic was assigned to one floor of a two story barracks. I knew everyone, but I had no particular buddy. It didn't really matter because we were kept very busy. We were assigned to Armament class on the swing shift. So the routine was sleep in to about 10 A.M., have a meal at the mess hall, come back to the barracks for two hours of calisthenics. Some free time, then about 4 P.M. have lunch, form up and march around the end of the runway to where the school was located. The class was eight hours, so about midnight we formed up, marched back around the runway to the mess hall for breakfast, then back to the barracks for sleep time.

The calisthenics were tough for a couple of weeks until I became used to the thin air of the mile high altitude. The chow at Lowery was great for this was a permanent Army Air establishment. The mess hall was in a large brick building, which also served as a cooks and bakers school. At the midnight meal, we were almost alone except for a few student cooks. Often there would be several apple pies set out on shelves to cool. These were in two by three foot baking tins, big pies. More than once, we managed to liberate one or two of these, sneaking them back to the barracks for our own little party.

I was only one week into this new school when disaster struck. Our group had earned our first weekend pass, so we all went into the big city. Upon my return Sunday evening, I found a note on my bunk. It read "call home immediately, death in the family." This was as if a lightning bolt struck. I raced out of the barracks and over to the PX where there were a couple of public telephones. I finally got through to home, State 5-4704. I still remember. I talked to my mother and learned that my younger sister Jeannie had collapsed and died that Sunday afternoon. I would have guessed anyone in the family but her because she was the picture of health.

I went back to my bunk and went to bed. Next morning I went to the Red Cross office and obtained verification of "death in the family." This I took to our headquarters building, asking to see the 1st Sergeant. Feeling quite sorry for myself when I was shown to his desk, I made the mistake of leaning over and placing my hands on the desk. The asshole came unglued and read me the riot act. I straightened up. When he was finished, I presented him with my problem along with the piece of paper from the Red Cross. He frowned, looked up at me and said, "You have ten days. Be back here in an hour to pick up your gate pass and travel papers." I started to argue that ten days was not enough, but he was already talking to someone else, ignoring me. From this time on, I hated 1st Sergeants.

I went back to the public telephone and called the railroad station for departure times to Los Angeles. The railroads during wartime are crowded with moving the military and do not really want to be bothered with single passengers. That's the answer I got from the ticket man on the telephone. He could not promise me a seat for a day or two. He did not care to hear about my emergency furlough. My next stop was the operations tower out on the airstrip. There I talked to the operations officer who was a real pal. He asked me if I had high altitude training. I had to tell him no. He said, "That's too bad as there is a flight of B17s coming here this afternoon, headed for March Field near Riverside. One other possibility, there is a VIP B25 headed for Mather AFB, near Sacramento. You might try him when he arrives." I beat it back to the barracks, packed my clothes, rushed over to headquarters to pick up my paper work, then out to the Control tower. I was none too soon for about 3 P.M. here comes this B25. It taxied right up to the front door and a couple of officers climbed out. The operations officer walked out and met the pilot, speaking to him about me needing a lift to California. He did this because there were others trying to hitch a ride, and this nice Captain wanted to see me get first chance. After talking to the pilot, he returned to where I was waiting and told me to go draw a parachute in a hurry. I drew a chute, rushed out to the plane and was told to climb in the rear. Inside the waist gunner's area was a Colonel sitting on an empty ammunition box. This was the VIP passenger. Since I was a lowly PFC, we did not have much conversation.

The pilot cranked up the engines, taxied out to the end of the runway, set the brakes and proceeded to run up each engine as this was AAF takeoff rules. Next came rev up both engines and release the brakes. What a thrill. That B25 pinned my stomach to my back bone with the acceleration. We were very soon airborne, headed west for California. I stayed by the Plexiglas window all the way, watching the mountains, then the desert, then more mountains. By late afternoon, we were over the Sierras. I recognized Lake Tahoe. Beautiful!! Soon after that we were approaching Mather Field. This B25 made a short trip of this. It was just turning dusk. After landing, I thanked the pilot and made for the gate and the highway. I stuck out my thumb and had a ride immediately. No problem at all hitchhiking when wearing a uniform. I was home next morning, surprising everyone when I came walking up. It was a very sad homecoming

My sister Jeannie, one and a half years younger than myself, had become a beautiful strawberry blonde. She was a very popular girl at school and had married a classmate of mine, Ted Miller, who had enlisted in the Navy. He was aboard a tramp steamer somewhere in the Pacific. The Navy would not, or maybe could not, contact him. There was no way to notify him of Jeannie's sudden death, other than sending a letter via the Navy San Francisco PO. Some day the letter would catch up with him at a port of call.

My Dad did not make it to the funeral either, which was held on Thursday. Following the funeral, the family went to dinner at a nice restaurant. We all tried to cheer my mom. She tried to be cheerful but would occasionally break into tears. I tried to stay close to her for the next few days, and then I got on the telephone, calling around to my friends. Everybody had gone into the service, most in the Navy. One day I went to the high school where IS ran across an old classmate, Russ Anderson. He was in uniform also, home on leave. In our conversation, I found out that he was also stationed at Lowery and would be returning there in a few days by train. We arranged to travel together.

"Sister Betty Marks & Bill"   *"PFC Bill Crum"*

The return to Lowery was uneventful. Upon my arrival, I was told I would have to wait two weeks for a new class to start. I was flabbergasted; I might as well have stayed at home for those two weeks. This was an example of the old Army proverb of "hurry up and wait." In this case, it was "hurry back and wait." On top of that, I would be classmates with a whole new group of students. The untimely death of my sister delayed my military education by at least a month. As it turned out, maybe this was a lifesaver for me.

The two weeks went by slowly. I found myself dodging KP duty. It was very difficult to loaf in your bunk all day, as some non-com was always policing the barracks looking for somebody goofing off from calisthenics, school or whatever. I got in the practice of finding an empty bunk, sometimes even in another barracks, where I would lie down to read. Then when the patrol came by to ask why I wasn't in class, I would say "sick call." He would get out his pencil and notebook and ask my name. I would answer, "Bill Monroe." He would jot that down and be off. Then I would get up and move to some other empty bunk just in case he hurried out to check on "Bill Monroe." I never did get caught.

Russ Anderson and I had made arrangements to go into the city together at the first opportunity. This took place on the following Saturday night. We met at the gate and rode the bus into Denver. The city was beautiful, for now it was fall with all of the tree lined streets in full color. Russ and I headed for a bar that he knew of. We each ordered a Zombie. The waitress brought out two tall glasses, with flames on top. I had never seen anything like it. I expected to land on the floor after consuming it. But we made this one round last all night. Then we got back on the bus and back to Lowery and went to bed. Not a real exciting evening. I never saw Russ again as he shipped out the next week.

The next Saturday night pass I was invited to my Uncle George Kriener's mother's home for dinner. My uncle had grown up in this house his mother informed me. It was a large two story brick, very elegant. George was a stock broker in Denver before retiring and moving to Van Nuys in the late '30s. He had somehow survived the big crash of the late '20s and was quite well off. He and my Aunt had always played Santa to the Crum kids in those lean years. Again, it was a pleasant but not very exciting Saturday night. I went back to Lowery, retiring early.

The next Monday, I was moved into a different barracks to be with the new class that was starting that evening. Some of us were sitting on the barracks porch killing time when two GI's in fatigues came running by. They were headed for the perimeter fence which was about 100 yards away. They reached the fence and went over it in one big hurry. About the time they jumped down on the outside, an MP came running by our porch. He was beat to a pulp, literally. He was making all sorts of guttural sounds but still managing to chase his prisoners. We later learned that he was guarding these two on a work detail in the laundry. The two sneaked a couple of GI soap bricks into a sack which they used for a hammer on the MP's head and face. This is a double whammy for the MP guard because not only does he endure the beating, he has to serve out his prisoners' sentence if they escape. There were some real mean people that were drafted into the service of our country. They invariably ended up in the stockade under guard.

Fall turned to Winter early in the year 1943. It began snowing which wasn't bad except for the long hike to class around the end of the runway. One night it was snowing heavily on our way back after class. A few of us decided to take a short cut and cross the runway for we felt sure there would not be any fool landing in this weather. This saved us a good half mile. No problem, except when we got to the other side and back on the perimeter road, here came two MP's in a Jeep. He did not have room in the Jeep for the six of us, so he got out his pencil and notepad and took down each man's name and s/n. He reported us to our Squadron Commander, so the next day each of us was called on the carpet. Each man got a lecture about the danger of crossing the runway on foot, and each of us was restricted to the base for the coming weekend. This is how I came to meet Dottie Rivard. This Saturday night that I was restricted, I went to an USO dance on the base. There were many unattached girls there because Denver was such a great city to the GI's. Most of the guys went into town on the weekends, leaving the local on-base dances uncrowded. Anyway, I picked Dottie, and we danced most of the dances. She told me that she was a bookkeeper at the local Armour meat plant. She had a brother in the service that was stationed in Cuba. I gave her a big line of BS about my life before being drafted. We hit it off well, so she invited me to her mother's house for dinner on my next pass. I accepted. The dance ended at midnight. Dottie left aboard a bus provided by the USO. She left me with her address and telephone number.

The next weekend I rode the bus into the city and walked to the address Dottie had given me. It was within walking distance of the city center in an old neighborhood. After I was introduced to her mother, the three of us had a nice dinner. Dottie and I then walked downtown to a movie. We talked of our favorite songs of the period. It was the big time of Frank Sinatra. He was Dottie's favorite. I did not care that much about him for he had all the teenage girls swooning over him. Besides, how was he avoiding the draft??

After that first week end in mid-October, I spent most every Saturday night with Dottie. We walked or rode the bus everywhere. There was only one problem: a 12 P.M. curfew in the city for GI's enforced by MP's. One Saturday night I overstayed at Dottie's house and was walking to the bus line as fast as I could. It was after the midnight curfew, so I was worried about getting nailed by the MP's. I was only a few steps beyond a parked sedan when someone inside rolled down the window and asked, "Hey, Soldier, want a ride?" I could not see inside the darkened interior except for the man who asked the question. He looked ok in the dark. I said, "Sure." I opened the back door and started to climb in. Out came a big middle aged lady who ushered me into the back seat where another big woman was seated on the far side. The first big lady climbed back in and closed the door. This put me squeezed in between two big fat cows that were up to no good, I could tell right away. There were two men in the front seat. The driver started the car and we drove off. I told them that I only needed a ride to the bus stop a few blocks away. They had other ideas, I never did figure out what. They were some kind of sex deviates and part of the women's conversation was "What do we do with Soldier boy?" I was very happy when they stopped the car and let me out. I would rather take my chances with the MP's. I made it to the bus and back to Lowery with no further problem. There were many nice people in Denver and generally the GI's were treated great, but this night I had met some of the bad. I was lucky to have escaped unscathed. I suspect I almost got raped or worse.

The weeks rolled by very rapidly. I was enjoying the learning experience. The more that I learned about aircraft, the more fascinated did I become. Most important, I was gaining confidence in myself as I was doing so well in the classroom, I surprised myself. I had never done this well in high school, in any subject.   .

I found the class on aircraft armament fascinating. We learned to be armament mechanics on bombers and fighters. This included 50 caliber Browning machine guns, which was the Air Force basic weapon, and 20 MM canon which some fighters used. All the bomber gun turrets were made by Sperry, Martin, Consolidated, and Emerson. We learned about bomb fuses, bomb sizes and purposes, bomb release mechanisms. For the first time in my life, I came to realize that I did have a brain in my head. I was at the head of the class all the way, in particular with any of the electric circuitry. There was only one other student that kept up with me, a 26 year old electrician from Illinois.

The Armament course took twelve weeks. When December 20th came around, we were graduated. There was not any ceremony but each man received another stripe—elevated to Corporal, which also meant an increase in pay. We were also given the opportunity to "volunteer" for flight duty. A few in the class were given a chance to go on with advanced armament in which the brand new central fire control system of the B29 was learned. I was one of the few, but I declined as I was now eager to fly. This was a big mistake which probably changed the course of my whole life. At the least, I would have fought the war in the Pacific instead of Europe because B29's were designed exclusively for the long flights to Tokyo. Besides, Dottie and I were getting pretty heavy on the week ends and no telling where that would have led had I stayed in school at Lowery for another six months. So I said my goodbyes. One week before Christmas I was loaded on a dilapidated troop train headed for flight gunnery school.

This trip turned out to be the most miserable train ride in my life. The train itself was of WW I vintage. Food was served, via mess kit, in an open box car with a wood burning cook stove in the middle. The chow line formed in the adjacent passenger car, single file into the cook car, past the wood stove where the cook slapped some food into your mess kit. There was no place to sit down to eat. No matter, because it did not take long to empty that mess kit with the train rocking and chugging along on the back roads of Oklahoma and East Texas. The temperature turned hot as we progressed slowly to the south. We were all in winter uniform for the cold snows of Denver. On about the third day, we reached Corpus Christy and had an hour lay over to change trains. A group of us left the train, heading to the nearest tavern to have a cold beer. We walked in with tongues hanging out, sat down at the bar and asked the lady bar tender for cold beer. She would not serve me or one of the others because we were not 21. I felt like tearing the place apart, but I refrained. To this day, I cannot say anything good about Texas.

The rest of our trip was aboard a different train. We arrived at Harlingen Texas, gunnery training school on the day before Christmas, 1943. We were settled into barracks and informed that we would be on KP Christmas day. Another strike for Texas! This turned out to be a memorable Christmas, up at dawn in time to serve breakfast, clean the plates and scrub the kitchen in time for the big turkey serving at midday. All is well so far, but that was soon to end. For dessert, ice cream was served in a paper wrapper which after the turkey and ice cream was devoured, was left on the tin cafeteria style tray. All of these paper wrappers ended up in the garbage cans out behind the kitchen where I was assigned to clean up. It was hot, and no one was happy about it being Christmas. A truck pulled up with an MP with a shotgun and two prisoners to pick up the garbage cans. The two prisoners hopped down off the truck and began shuffling the big cans around in preparation for loading them onto the truck bed. One of these characters spotted the papers mixed in with the garbage and began swearing at me like as if I had put them there. He said something about the hog's can't eat paper, and I said something back. This lit his fuse, and he swore some more and took a swing at my face. I was taken completely by surprise, but I still managed to duck just enough to the right so his fist only grazed my left ear. The MP jumped down from the truck and muscled this punk to the ground. I went about my KP duties. A couple of days later, I was called into the MP office and asked some questions about the event. I presume the guy received some extra time in the stockade for taking that poke at me.

Gunnery school was great. It consisted of some classroom studies, mostly precautions and rules for handling weapons. Also, a day was spent learning about high altitude and its affect on the body. The morning was classroom lecture, and the afternoon the class was ushered into the high altitude chamber where we sat on benches placed along the sides. The door was closed and the pumps turned on to evacuate the air. At the simulated altitude of 10,000 feet, the instructor told us to put on the oxygen mask provided for each student. We were told that this was an Air Force regulation--at 10,000 feet and above, wear your oxygen mask. The chamber was pumped down to simulate 25,000 feet. Then the instructor went to each student one at a time and turned off the oxygen. In this way, all the rest of the students could observe the effect. It took about two minutes after the oxygen was turned off for the student to become unconscious. His head falls, and he slumps over. The instructor immediately opens a supply valve to turn the oxygen back on. The student slowly recovers without even knowing he had been out. This demonstrates the danger of flying at high altitude for if somehow you become disconnected from the pressurized oxygen supply tanks, you will become unconscious without feeling a thing wrong. If six minutes goes by, you become very dead.

For the most part, the training consisted of shooting everything from shotguns to machine guns. Almost every hour of every day was spent on the firing range. We rode around an oval track on a flatbed truck shooting at clay pigeons thrown in our direction. They mounted shot guns in gun turrets and threw clay pigeons at you. I had my first ride in a B24. There were about ten of us students crowded into the waist gun position. We each had a turn at the ball turret. That was a memorable experience. A couple of the students came out of there white as a sheet. I think that spelled the end of their flight gunnery training. Another exciting day on the flight line was a ride in the rear seat of an AT6 which was equipped with a 30 caliber machine gun. After reaching about 5000 ft. out over Padre Island, a tow target came by. We were instructed to shoot at it.

As at Lowery, I was a very good student, interested in all of the activities. One day in a class of about twenty, there were two 2nd Lieutenants from Infantry. The instructor was a non-com back from the air war in Europe. He was supposed to be passing to us the benefits of his combat experience. He was telling us to always eyeball the 50 caliber guns before climbing into the airplane to make sure the mechanics had not left a rag stuffed in the end of the barrel. If you got out on the mission and fired that gun, the rag, or any other foreign object, would cause the gun to explode. I was thinking, so I asked the instructor, what happens when ice forms in the barrel, and it is fired. One of the smart ass officer-students answered my question before the instructor had a chance to speak. He said, "There isn't moisture enough at high altitude to form ice." I then asked, "Why do the bombers have de-icing boots on wing and tail leading edges?" That was apparently beyond the Lieutenant's intelligence level for he came back with a sharp, "Don't argue with an officer." This ended the question and answer session. The instructor promptly moved on to another subject.

I was still mad at Texas for the episode at Corpus Christy so I chose to remain on the base on the weekends. Some of my fellow students went on weekend pass to Mattamoris across the border in Mexico, and they came back with some wild tales about girlie shows. I was writing to Dottie. Via the mail, we were becoming thicker, so I was not interested in any dirty "girlie shows." Besides, across the border, it was alive with Gonorrhea and the like, according to the instructors. That also was part of our training at Harlingen. We had classes on VD, and its prevention. They showed movies demonstrating what Syphilis and Gonorrhea do if the preventions are ignored. I did not want any part of it, so I spent my leisure time on the base at the PX drinking beer and sitting on the grass. Because it was warm here in the middle of January, everyone wore summer uniforms.

February came and our class was graduated. We each received another stripe and were issued gunner's wings to wear. Also I was given a ten day delay in route, which amounted to ten days at home in route to my next station which was to be Westover Field, Massachusetts. After the graduation, I was packing my bag getting ready to leave. When I took my shower, I left my uniform laid out on my bunk along with my brand new wings. I came back from the shower to find that some bum had stolen my wings. I was real pissed. I went to the PX on the way to the bus and purchased another.

"Gunnery School Graduation"

I had been writing to Dottie every few days and receiving a letter from her most every day. We were going at it as hot and heavy as the mail allowed. Sometime in

January I asked her to meet me at my home on my upcoming ten day furlough. She agreed to the idea, writing that she would take her vacation at that time. So here it was February. I was on my way home on my first leave since being in the Service. I had progressed to Sergeant, was sporting flight crew gunner's wings and was on my way to Westover to start flight training. On top of that, I would be seeing my family and my best girl. I was sitting on top of the world.

The trip to Los Angeles was uneventful. I do not remember much except at one stop, someplace out in the middle of Texas; we passengers were out on the loading platform stretching our legs. There were about six MP's with Thompson submachine guns surrounding a group of newly captured German prisoners from the tank war going on in North Africa. This was my first glimpse of the real war. The Germans were all young, like me, and obviously they were not too happy. Little did I know that in approximately one year from this time, I would find myself in the exact reverse situation at Frankfort, Germany.

My great sister Betty met me at the train station in downtown LA in her '41 Olds. We drove to Van Nuys-- my mother's old house where I had been born. I had never really appreciated that old house until now. It looked great after the months of Army barracks. And most of the family was home: Betty and Grace with their new babies, Eddie JR and tiny Carole; my Aunt Grace and Uncle George from Denver; Bob and sister Helen, with their two kids, Duane and Leni. The only ones missing were two brothers-in-law, Ed Marks and Fred Place, both of whom were in the Navy someplace. And my Dad and sister Jeannie were missed by all.

The second day home, Dottie was due to arrive at the same down town train station, so sister Betty and I drove in her car to pick her up. It was about an hour drive those days because there were no freeways. The short route was through Hollywood and follow Sunset or Melrose or one of them with their stop and goes traffic signals, all the way to Main Street in LA. Fortunately there was not too much traffic because gasoline was strictly rationed. I don't know where Betty was getting hers. Anyway, we met Dottie and returned home. My mother found someplace for her to sleep, and I moved out to my old shed bedroom. It was raining hard the whole ten days, with minor flooding, so we were confined to indoors mostly. My mother had a family gathering on Sunday to celebrate my being home and my nineteenth birthday.

One night, Dottie and I were invited to dinner at Bob and Helen's new home in North Hollywood. Another night we double dated with my old buddy Milt Mistich who was the only one of my old friends who was not in the Service. He was in and out already, declared unfit because of his asthma. I had a very good time for the whole ten days. Dottie pressured me to get married, but I resisted. She settled for an engagement ring. I had never thought about getting married.

When the ten days were up, Betty took Dottie and me to the train station. I had my ticket purchased by the Army. Dottie was able to get on the same train as far as Cheyenne, where she would change to go south to Denver. I would continue on the same train to Chicago where I would change and head north towards Massachusetts. This arrangement gave us a couple of more days together, albeit on a train seat that we shared. The train was crowded, so we had an audience all the time so we couldn't get too serious about necking. We arrived in Cheyenne, said our good byes, and went our separate ways. The rest of the train ride for me was pretty miserable. It seemed that the further east we traveled, the more crowded the train became. There were many war brides, some with bawling babies. The war separated thousands of families. It seemed everyone was always saying goodbye. I wasn't ready for this part of it.

The train finally arrived in Chicago. I grabbed my bag and departed. Out on the platform, I was shocked to see trains coming from the east, with three foot icicles hanging from the cars. Here I was in summer uniform. I found my train going to Springfield, Massachusetts, and climbed aboard. This train was more crowded than the last. But I found an empty seat, stowed my duffel bag of clothes, sat down, and went to sleep. This was the last leg of my journey clear across the country, and I was tiring.

Early in the morning I arrived in Springfield where it was clear and cold. I remember walking down the street from the train station, looking up at a B24 cruising overhead in the clear blue sky at about 20,000 feet. I shuddered to think how cold it must be up there, and I expected that I would be up there soon.

Westover Field was about ten miles east of Springfield. I checked in and was assigned barracks and a bunk. I found that I knew a number of the people, as the whole barracks were filled with gunners and armament techs. A couple of days went by, then a large group of pilots, co-pilots, navigators, bombardiers, radio operators, engineers, armorers and gunners were all gathered in a big hanger. The officer in charge started with the pilots, calling their names in alphabetical order. Then a co-pilot was assigned to each pilot, and then a navigator and so on until each pilot had a ten man crew of each of the specialties. My pilot was Lt. Al Berthelsen, co-pilot Lt. Tom Riggles, navigator Lt. Herb Gilliam, bombardier Lt. Don Maslow, Radio Keith Holdredge, engineer Charles Spivey, armorer myself, and three gunners, Willie Pounds, Donald Johnson and Louis Winter. We introduced ourselves to each other, and sized each other up. The pilot co-pilot combination was sort of "Mutt and Jeff" as Berthelsen was a little short guy while Riggles was big and tall. In the coming months, they learned to make a great team in the cockpit of the B24. Holdredge was the oldest in the crew at twenty-eight years. He was partially bald. Spivey was from Georgia with that southern drawl. Pounds was from New Orleans. Johnson was a tall skinny kid from Minnesota. Winter was a stocky built kid from Mississippi. Berthelsen, Spivey and Pounds were married. These were the old men on the crew, all in their mid-twenties.

"Berthelsen Crew   Westover Field"

The training consisted of some classroom lectures of various subjects such as how to use a parachute, how to avoid VD, etc. Many classes were held in a darkened room for recognition practice of friendly and enemy aircraft and ships. Then some more VD lectures, like they were the most important of all.

We made many training flights, some just navigator practice, some simulated bombing runs on a target city. One trip was for gunnery practice in which we flew low over the Nantucket area, and I practiced strafing a target dropped on the water. That was a thrill, skimming the water in that ball turret. We also flew some high altitude training flights. Sometimes an instructor would accompany our crew, but most of the time we were on our own. We were doing well, no goof ups. Some crews had to put in extra hours after making mistakes. Landings were observed by the operations tower, and if somebody screwed up too many times, they were required to make some "touch and go" landings for an hour or so. One day we were on the runway approach waiting our turn to move onto the runway and take off. One of the crews doing the touch and go routine, touched down on the runway right in front of us. He stayed on the ground for a distance, and then gave it the gun to take off and go around again. But something went wrong. He left the ground with insufficient air speed and a half mile off the end of the runway the left wing went down. The plane went into the ground with a ball of flame and column of smoke. We later learned that three men died-- pilot, co-pilot and instructor pilot.

I was having one big adventure. Every day was a learning experience. We were treated really great on the base, no KP, no latrine duty, no policing the area (picking up cigarette butts). Our pilot was our boss, and all of our scheduling came down through him. When there was nothing scheduled, we were free to go into town or whatever. Since the number of aircraft was limited, and there were about twenty student crews in the group, we had to take turns. This left plenty of free time. One day, I stuffed my fleece lined jacket into a duffel bag and caught the bus to Springfield. There I found a photographer, put on the leather flight jacket, and posed for a picture, complete with silk scarf. I had several made, sending them home to the family. I was very proud of those photos. At home, there was a picture of my Dad in sailor's uniform, taken in Boston around 1900 when he was in the Navy for the Spanish-American War. This photo of me in flight gear gave me the feeling of comradeship with my Dad. I was proud of us both.

One day, while waiting in the chow line, I ran into Bill Hennes. He was one of the original draftees from the Los Angeles area that I was with through Basic at Kearns, Utah. He had also gone to Armament at Lowery at the same time I had. Then I got behind him when I got the emergency furlough. I had encountered him one night on the street in Denver while out with Dottie. He was about to complete training there and move on to gunnery school. Now, here he was, about to complete training at Westover, still a couple of months ahead of me but on the same track. I was to meet up with him again some months later, like I was following him. We both had the same destiny.

I joined my friends and went into town on Friday nights. I tried staying true to Dottie, but it did not work. There were too many girls looking for men and a good time. They came to Springfield on the weekends from all over because of Westover and all of the GI's. I telephoned Dottie and told her the engagement was off. I could not stand it. Subsequent to that, my buddy Bob Clarke and I were hitchhiking on our way into Springfield on a bright warm Sunday when a '37 Ford sedan with four girls picked us up. They were good lookers, on their way home from church. They put me in the front seat between two and Bob in the back seat between two. We were introduced all around, and then drove toward Springfield. I was catering to the driver, Joanne, mostly because I liked the car. She asked Bob and me if we would like to accompany them to a dance that evening. We accepted, agreeing to meet someplace later in the day. So about seven that evening, we met and drove into a little town in Connecticut. When we were still two blocks from the dance hall, we could hear the music and the stomping of feet. It was then that I learned that Joanne was Polish and that the dance was all polka. Oh well, it was fun trying. I did a good job of getting in everybody's way. Joanne tried to teach me the step, but I was having trouble. She was very patient.

It was while taking a break at one end of the hall that I learned that my hearing was going downhill with all of the machine gun and flight activity. Joanne looked around searching for the source of a telephone ringing. She said, "I wonder where that telephone is?" I said, "What telephone?" She said, "Don't you hear that telephone?" I didn't hear a thing except for the music and all that stomping of feet.

Joanne returned Bob and me to Westover that night, leaving us off at the gate. We made a date to meet the next weekend. The next weekend led to the following weekend, and the next after that. I met her family one afternoon. She had an older sister and a younger brother. Her mother and father were from the old country, speaking broken English. They lived in the township of Chicopee Falls, in a small apartment building facing the Connecticut River. Taking off from Westover headed west, the bombers followed the river so at times it could get pretty noisy. Joanne's mother complained to me a couple of times about that, like as if I could do something about it. Turn off the war maybe?

"Ball Turret Training"

Our training progressed through the months. Towards the middle of June, it was mostly the pilot and co-pilot getting in the minimum flight hours in the cockpit.

Much of this time, Lt. Berthelsen, nice guy that he was, did not require all of us to go along. So that meant more time off, several days during the week as well as the week end. This meant more time with Joanne. Come the 4th of July, the family invited me to go with them to a nearby lake for a picnic. We all crowded into that '37 Ford. It was a great day, with lots of beer. Joanne's dad had me chasing beer with a straight shot of bourbon. He said that was the custom where he came from. It was a beautiful small lake, and the weather was just right for a picnic. Everybody had a good time.

"Fourth of July Picnic 1944"

The second week of July our training was completed. We were loaded up with shots, dental work completed, full clothing and flight equipment issued, final physical completed. Each made out a will, so all the preparations were made for a long stay overseas. Then we were given a seven day leave and told to be back on time or it would be considered desertion as we were now fully trained and headed for combat.

What could I do with seven days? No way could I make it to California and back. I went out to the operations tower to check on maybe getting a ride. There was not anything to California, but there was a B24 would be leaving in an hour for Denver. I hunted down the pilot to ask him about a ride to Denver. He said OK, be back here at 1300 hours. I decided to risk it, so I hurried back to the barracks to pack a bag. The next stop was a scheduled pep talk from the base C/O. He told us we were the best trained air crews in the world. And he wished us luck and happy hunting. While he went on and on about how good we were, through the open hanger door, I watched my ride to Denver speeding down the runway. Well, that's the way the ball bounces. No telling how my life would have changed had I made it to Denver.

When the lecture was over, we were dismissed to leave. I told the others in my crew of my missed ride out of there. The bombardier from New York had a car. He was heading that way, and I could have a ride. So a buddy and I crowded into the car to see the big city. We stayed at the "Y" in New York. We climbed to the top of the Empire State Bldg. We rode the ferry out to the Statue of Liberty, climbing to the top. We rode the subway out to Brooklyn and Coney Island. I went to Mitchell Field and looked up a friend. We went to Jack Dempsey's Bar to have a couple of drinks. We went to a "dime a dance" place where the dancing partners were some old bags in evening gowns. Every time the music stopped, they held out their hand for another dime. No dime, no dance. What a racket. In fact, servicemen received no breaks in the Big Apple. On the contrary, it seemed that somebody was always holding their greedy hand out for a tip. So I saw quite a bit of New York City on my seven day leave.

At least I didn't have to worry about getting back to Westover on time. In fact I was a day early so went to see Joanne and say my good-byes. It was a good thing that I did, for one day after our return we packed our bags, and along with five other crews, boarded a train. Destination was Langley Field, Virginia. We traveled as a crew now, and upon arrival at Langley, the enlisted men bunked together.

At this base, we were originally scheduled to get six weeks of super secret radar bombing training. But before we could get started, an urgent call for replacements crews came in. We were told to repack our bags and be ready to go. Maslow would remain at Langley for the radar training. We were not told where we would be going, but we had a good idea. D Day in France was just past and lots of replacement air crews were needed. Never the less, Berthelsen held a conference and took a vote. If we were given a choice, would we take Europe or the Pacific war? We all agreed that the Pacific would be best. For me it would probably mean I would see home before going overseas. Anyway, we were issued a brand new B24, complete with radar bombing equipment. We took it on a test flight over Chesapeake Bay. A gasoline leak developed in the wing main fuel tanks, so we returned to Langley real fast.

We were given another physical. In the eye test, I was having trouble reading the wall chart with my left eye. A sergeant medic and I were alone in this room where the eye tests were given. When I couldn't pass I think he thought that I was faking it to avoid combat. He looked puzzled and asked how I got this far with bad eyesight. I told him that I had just got off a dirty train and had coal dust in my eye and had been rubbing it. He bought that answer and wrote 20/20 down on my record. The fact is I never had another eye exam after the induction center in Los Angeles where they were so anxious to fill the manpower quotas. They were not too careful.

It was hot and sweaty at this time at Langley. I remember standing in the chow line with sweat pouring off of everyone. We were still there over the weekend because of repairs to our gas leak. So four of us decided to go into Newport News and have a cold beer. It turns out no taverns open on Sunday, so we bought a six pack and went to the nearby park where there was plenty of shade. We found a spot and got comfortable on the grass. Each had a can of beer. We noticed some civilians walking by giving us some dirty looks, but we did not pay much attention. A short time later, a cop came up and said, "It is against the law to consume alcohol in public. You boys come with me." We were flabbergasted, but we went with him to the local police station where he called the MP's. They arrived, hauled us back to Langley, wrote down each man's name, and said we would hear from their office later. We did not tell him that we were leaving town as soon as our plane was ready. The people were terrible here to all the GI's, on and off the base. We had another fiasco in the barracks. We had upstairs bunks. We were sitting there sorting and packing our gear when we heard someone stomping up the stairs. We did not pay any attention until this Army Captain was beside us hollering, "Who is going to call attention around here?" He proceeded to read us the riot act. He chewed us up one side and down the other for ignoring an officer's presence. He also took our names and said we would be disciplined. Fortunately, we loaded into our plane the next day and left for an airbase in New Hampshire. We all got a big laugh out of that, including Berthelsen. That's the way it was in the Army Air Force in those days. Most of the ground forces resented the Air Corps way back to the days of Billy Mitchell, and every chance they rubbed it in. An enlisted man had to be very careful when at a station where there were regular Army officers around.

This was a brand new B24, destined to be a lead ship. It had all this super secret radar bombing equipment installed on the flight deck. The bombardier and navigator had the equipment turned on and were playing with it. No one aboard knew how to operate it for real but at least had the scope on and the sweep antenna going. We took turns observing the image on the screen. I happened to have my turn just as we passed over Long Island, N.Y. I observed the shoreline very clearly.

Then I shifted my gaze out the Plexiglas bubble and looked down. There straight below was the same shoreline that I was seeing on the screen. Fascinating!

We landed at this base in New Hampshire where we were put up in quarters provided for transients. Next morning we were issued survival equipment which consisted of sleeping bags, carbine rifles, fishing tackle, C rations, maps. This was ten of each (ten man crew) so plywood decking was installed in the bomb bay to accommodate all this stuff. Then we were gassed up, and Lt. Berthelsen was given a sealed envelope with instructions not to open until airborne. This was tough on him because he was leaving behind a wife who was nine months pregnant. He would have liked nothing better than to get on the telephone to tell her of our destination.

Shortly after we took off, the sealed orders were read. As was suspected, we were headed for England, with the first stop being Goose Bay, Labrador. This was a real adventure to me. I stood at the waist window for hours, watching the Canadian wilderness with the hundreds of lakes. We were in the air for a good six hours that first day, landing at Goose Bay late in the afternoon. But this was late July, and we were in the far north, so the days were long. The other five crews traveling with us had already arrived, so their planes were being serviced when we taxied onto the ramp and parked.

We were treated like royalty here. The base was maintained by MATS (Military Air Transport Command), and they were very efficient. Also they welcomed our business. I guess they were lonely, stuck off here in this wild country. One of the truck drivers took a truck load of us on a tour of the countryside, to the end of the road that is. The surrounding growth consisted of small fir, like Christmas trees. The nearby stream that the road followed looked gray, like from a glacier. It was all very interesting. We returned to the base, had chow and went to bed.

Next morning we were out on the runway early. Lt. Berthelsen was in a big hurry now to get to our ultimate destination, so that he would have an address to mail to his wife. She in turn could respond to let him know that he was a father of what—boy or girl. Since the ground crews were at a minimum, we were pretty much on our own. We did all the preliminaries ourselves, like walking the props through a couple of turns. The other crews were on the parking strip doing the same. The pilots were having some conversation, apparently dreaming up a bet on who was going to get to the next stop first. Lt. Berthelsen came running, motioning for us to climb in fast. He got in the cockpit, cranked up the engines, gave them minimum warm up, moved out on the ramp towards the runway and made a running takeoff. That is he turned onto the runway at taxi speed, aimed the nose and pushed the throttles all the way. I was standing between pilot and co-pilot, observing the cockpit operation.

We were about halfway down the runway when Riggles sensed something wrong as he looked at the engine instruments, noting low manifold pressure. He blurted out, "Goddammit Al!" He reached over and pushed on the four turbo's. As the B24 increased speed we left the ground just in time to clear the fir trees at the end of the runway. We could have been splattered all over those trees due to "PILOT ERROR."

Our next scheduled stop was Iceland. The route there took us over Greenland. I looked out the waist window, observing that these two island countries were named backwards. Greenland was all mountains, ice and glaciers, while Iceland was relatively flat with at least some green. We flew directly over a giant glacier with huge crevasses. It was very forbidding looking territory. I also saw many icebergs floating on the North Atlantic. This was a long flight, so when I got tired of standing, I sat down on the deck and joined the others playing black-jack.

We landed at Reykjavik, Iceland, where we were put up for the night in transient quarters. It was still broad daylight at 11 P.M. The barracks had heavy blackout shutters on all of the windows to enable one to sleep. We hit the sack early as there was not much to see here. Anyway, Lt. Berthelsen informed us that we would be leaving early in the morning. But it did not work out that way. We were out on the airstrip early alright, but our B24 had problems. It had been refueled to maximum capacity, and the aircraft had tipped down onto the tail-skid. That disclosed a problem in the main fuel tanks as gasoline was dripping out of the wing into the bomb bay. This was a very dangerous problem, and we had come halfway across the North Atlantic with it. The ground crew towed the plane to the maintenance area. They informed us that they knew exactly what the problem was because this was not the first brand new B24 that showed up there with the same problem, which was fuel tank vent hose clamps not installed properly. The problem is, to gain access to those hose clamps, the wing had to be opened up, the rubber tanks collapsed and removed. This was a big job. It would take MATS minimum maintenance crew, a week to make this repair. Berthelsen was fit to be tied. He told his father-to-be story to the maintenance chief who said he would furnish the tools and supervise, if we would do the work. That way we might get it done in a day or so.

This turned out to be my only mechanical work on a B24 in my entire Air Force career. We all pitched in with screwdrivers, removing the hundreds of fasteners on the bottom side of the wing. It was no problem working a twenty hour day outside with all of the daylight. We got the wing apart and went to bed very tired. Next morning we went back to continue, but the maintenance crew had jumped on it and completed the job. I think Berthelsen must have bribed them. Anyway, it was fixed. The tanker truck pulled alongside and filled the main tanks again. We gathered our gear, climbed aboard and took off. Berthelsen was happy to be on the way again. Our destination this time was a modification depot in Wales.

Again we flew for hours over the North Atlantic. Because there was nothing to see, I joined in the blackjack game with Winter, Pounds and Johnson. Mostly we flew at around 6000 ft., so it was not too uncomfortable. Our route took us over Ireland where we dropped down to 1000 ft to get under the cloud cover. I observed that the countryside was very green. The navigator was continuously plotting our course and calling out landmarks to the pilot as we had been warned not to depend on the radio compass. The Germans sometimes managed to warp the airwaves and could steer an unwary crew right into occupied France and captivity. What an obnoxious trick.

We landed at the mod center in Wales just before dusk. We were met by an officer and directed to unload all of our gear out onto the concrete apron. It turned out that they were more anxious to get this radar equipped plane on its way to the war zone than the crew. They wasted no time in towing the plane off to a hanger. We stood on the apron until a truck picked us up and hauled us to the mess hall. Our pile of survival gear remained out there on the concrete. We never saw it again.

CHAPTER V

JOINING THE BIG WAR

We were taken by truck to a replacement depot in England. The officers went one place while the six of us enlisted men were put up in this ex-woman's dormitory. It was horrible--with bathtubs instead of showers. It was out in the country, and we were restricted to the area. We waited here close to three weeks before being assigned to the 389th Bomb Group. Subsequent to being assigned, we were trucked to an airfield, and then flown to an advanced gunnery school on the coast of Ireland. This was my one and only ride in a B17; it had been converted to troop carrier duty.

We gunners spent two weeks at this place. We had some classroom studies, consisting of German tactics, and much aircraft recognition as the P51 escort fighter was easily mistaken for the German ME109. We also spent time on the firing range which consisted of a ball turret hung from a tripod support, placed on the beach fifty yards from the water's edge. We lined up behind the turret. Each man took a turn climbing into the turret, then firing at a tow target passing by out over the water. The two fifty caliber machine guns inside that turret were deafening. This is where my hearing suffered, never to recover.

When our two weeks were up, we were loaded into GI trucks, with all of our baggage into a trailer that was towed behind. A couple of the group decided to ride in the trailer, sprawled out on top of the baggage. There was a light mist falling, just enough to wet down the road. We were headed down the road going toward Belfast. Our driver was not experienced in driving on the left side of the road, so when he met a car coming the other way, he turned sharply to the other lane, then back to the right lane, then back to the left and finally back to the right. The trailer was being whipped from side to side, sliding on the wet pavement with the two passengers hanging on for dear life. They were petrified. At the final swing, we went up over the curb and came to a halt against a stone wall. The left front wheel of the truck had run over the front end of the little civilian car and squashed it. There were several passengers in the car. The two in the back seat were OK, but very shook up. The front seat passengers were not so well off. I have no idea what became of them as we had a boat to catch and did not wait for an ambulance. An officer traveling with us stayed with the wreck. No one in the truck or trailer was hurt. We continued on the road to Belfast encountering one more delay just outside of the city. That was a funeral procession, which was very impressive. It consisted of a beautiful horse drawn full glass carriage with maybe fifty people following behind. The black horses leading the procession had all silver harness. The carriage was shiny black, with much silver trim. The driver sat on top dressed in black. The casket, surrounded with flowers, lay inside visable through the windows. Then all of the mourners followed on foot, the whole procession proceeding slowly up the little hill toward the cemetery. We were able to watch the whole thing as all highway activity was stopped in respect for the funeral.

The convoy of about six trucks, each with their baggage trailer, proceeded through the streets of Belfast to the harbor. There we boarded a ferry which took us to Liverpool where we transferred to a train which in turn took us to Norwich. There we were met by a truck from the 389th Bomb Group based at the village of Hethel. Our long journey was finally over. Arriving at Hethel we were met by 566th officers who assigned us to quarters--the officers to theirs and we six enlisted to ours.

The barracks were British style Quonset huts. In fact, the air base itself was originally occupied by the British in the early days of the war. There were the enlisted personnel of six crews to each hut, thirty-six men. The beds were double bunks lined up on each side of the building, with the foot towards the isle which ran down the center. At the far end of the isle, there was an undersized pot-bellied stove for heat. The latrine, with showers, was outside the entrance door in a small out building. Our hut was out among ancient oak trees, some distance from the mess hall, headquarters, and all the rest of the establishment. This was an ex-RAF air station, laid out in the early days of the air battles over Briton, when the Germans were frequent visitors. So everything, including the aircraft parking aprons, was dispersed into the woods as much as possible. There were no two buildings or aircraft lined up in a neat row like back in the states. This was for the protection against air attack as we were in the war zone now. Also, all of the windows in all of the buildings had black out curtains which were kept closed at night.

This was to be home for the duration of the war, or for our assigned tour of duty, which ever came first. At this period of the air war, the German Luftwaffe was pretty well beaten. The ball turrets of all B24's were removed in favor of weight and airspeed. The tour of duty for the bomber crews was now thirty-five missions. It was originally twenty-five when the 8th started daylight bombing of the continent in late 1942. You had to be lucky to survive twenty-five back then because German fighters were meeting the bombers every mission. Then as time went on the 8th received more and more fighter escort, and there became fewer and fewer German fighters. The tour of duty was first increased to thirty missions. After D Day, it was increased to thirty-five, just in time for us.

The other five crews in the barracks were at various stages in their tour. We moved in and wasted no time in becoming acquainted. They helped us newcomers by showing us around to the mess hall, the briefing room, church, etc. We were pretty much on our own once assigned to quarters. Most all communications was with the operations and was handed down via Lt. Berthelsen and a bulletin board posted at the entrance to the mess hall. We were issued flight gear, helmet, oxygen mask, maewest, electric heated suit, silk gloves, fur lined boots, parachute and a 45 automatic pistol in a shoulder holster. Last, we were assigned a locker to keep all the equipment in.

Standing left to right:

Holdredge   Winter   Johnson   Pounds   Spivey   Crum

Kneeling left to right:

Faircloth   Riggles   Muskrat   Berthelsen

Bill Faircloth, bombardier, assigned to our crew. Gwillim,

our navigator, left us to become a lead crew Navigator

About a week went by before we were alerted to fly a mission. This first one turned out to be for practice. The whole group was being introded to jet fighters which the Luftwaffe was beginning to use. We took off, formed into normal formation but stayed over England while P51's play-attacked. Then a British jet made the scene to show what he could do. The gunners tracked the fighters but fired no bullets. It was a very realistic exercise lasting a couple of hours, then back to Hethel. After landing, Johnson, in the nose turret, got airsick. This is an impossible situation with the necessity of wearing an oxygen mask to stay alive. Also, there is not room in the turret to carry a bucket and there were no plastic bags those days. So on the truck ride back to de-briefing, I volunteered to trade positions with Johnson. He would take my waist gun position, while I would take the nose turret. This turned out to be a fatal mistake for Johnson and a life-saver for me.

A few more days went by and then we were alerted via the bulletin board to fly our first real mission. The date was August 30th 1944, 389th mission no.188. We hit the sack early in anticipation of a big day ahead.

The mission begins with somebody shining a flashlight in your face, simultaneously shaking you awake. It was just turning daylight. I hurried into my long johns and outer clothing. The other five members of our crew were doing the same. We walked together to the mess hall and were served a great breakfast, except for the powdered milk. I could never get used to that. After breakfast it was briefing. Here all of the crews flying this mission are assembled in a theatre style room. The operations officer gets up on the stage at the front of the room and using a pointer, on a huge wall map, outlines the route to and from the target. He talks about the bomb type and size that would be carried, also the expected German defenses. He tells us the time of arrival over the target and the expected time back to Hethel. He talks for half an hour, passing on all of the intelligence known of the target. This day, the target was V1 launch sites at Pas de Calais, France. The V1's were unmanned drones loaded with explosives. They were launched and pointed toward London usually. They flew until they ran out of fuel, then look out below. They nose-dived into the ground and exploded on impact. They were hard on the nerves of the people of London as they made a weird sound as they put-put-put-along overhead. Then when the sound stopped, the people on the ground below had better dive for cover.

The briefing ends with a prayer led by Father Beck. He was a Catholic priest, white haired, in his mid fifties. He was well known and well liked around Hethel. Our next activity consisted of a short walk to the locker room where we each suited up with our new issue of equipment. This took about fifteen minutes. Then we step outside where we meet with Lt. Berthelsen, Lt.Riggles, and newly assigned bombardier Lt Faircloth. Our navigator, Lt. Gwillam, was taken from our crew so for the time being, we would fly with a nine man crew. When we are all present and accounted for, we climb aboard a GI truck and head for the assigned B24. Being a new crew, we did not have a permanent assigned aircraft, instead we flew the spares. Some of them were well used, but we had no say in the matter.

Arriving at our B24, we climbed off the truck and into the aircraft via the bomb-bay. This time it is a tight squeeze as the bombs are loaded. In fact the plane is fueled, ammunition loaded and it is ready to go as the ground crews work through the night preparing the bombers for this assigned mission. The crew sorts itself out, six to the flight deck and four to the waist. This is the take off routine. The pilot receives word via radio to start engines, and they are cranked up one at a time. With all four engines running, we move slowly out of the parking strip, taxi down the ramp and get in line with all of the other bombers. The control tower is visible now and each B24 awaits a green flare fired from the front porch. From here on, it is radio silence. The take off is precarious for the bomber is loaded to capacity. Any error in the cockpit or mechanical failure can cause a catastrophe. We use the entire 5,000 foot runway, leaving the ground just in time to clear the old oak trees on the far end of the runway.

This day is clear and sunny. We circle and climb, circle and climb. This is a short mission, with a south west heading, crossing the channel just south of London. To avoid German anti-aircraft fire as much as possible, the general rule was never enter enemy air space at less than 20,000 feet. For this short trip across the channel, that meant we had to get to 15,000 feet before heading south. Subsequent to reaching that altitude, I gathered my chute and headed for the bomb-bay. I climb through and stow the chute in front of the forward bulkhead. Then I proceed to pull the safety pins on each of the bombs. When this chore is completed, I climb forward through the tunnel past the retracted nose wheel, into the navigator/bombardier compartment. I stow my chute under the nose turret and climb in. By now, at 15000 feet, I am pooped, running very short on oxygen, so I waste no time putting on my oxygen mask and connecting the hose to the regulator. Then I connect my microphone and headset and check in with the pilot as follows, "Nose turret to pilot-bomb arming has been completed." Now I can settle back to enjoy the scenery.

Our course took us close to London, a huge city spread out all over many square miles. There must have been a thousand barrage balloons tethered over the city. Soon we passed out over the channel. The pilot calls on the intercom "test fire all guns." So each gun position, usually one at a time, fires a short burst. When Winter is firing from the tail turret, I can feel the shaking clear up in the nose turret.

It does not take long to cross the channel and the coast of France. This part is now occupied by U.S. ground forces, so we don't have to worry about anti aircraft fire. We make a big circle and come over the target area from the south. It is beautiful bombing weather, only a few scattered clouds far below. I strained my eyes trying to pick out the V1 launch ramps, but the Germans must have them camouflaged. I was still looking down when the lead plane dropped their bombs. This was the signal for the rest of the twelve planes to drop. The bombardier calls out "bombs away" on the intercom and the B24 lurches up and forward with the relief from the weight of several tons of the bomb-load. Now the Germans let loose with a few 88 rounds, but they burst not even close. The formation turned away from the target and was out over the channel in a minute. I was thinking to myself, "This is duck soup. What a great way to fight a war!"

Crossing back over the channel, I was able to spot the White Cliffs of Dover. The formation dropped altitude and when back over England I am permitted to leave my turret and return to the waist area where it was more comfortable. From there it was only a half hour flight back to Hethel. Since we were low on the totem pole in seniority, we were placed "tail end Charlie" in the formation so we circled around several times waiting our turn to land. This was neat in nice weather as we could look down into people's backyards. It was always a treat to fly at tree top level. This is the war zone, and the minimum 2000 foot altitude rule in the states did not apply.

After landing and parking the plane at its parking ramp, we wait for the engines to stop Then each gathered his gear, exited the plane down through the bomb-bay where usually a truck awaited to haul us back to de-briefing. This was held in a large open room with several tables, one table for each crew. First stop here is a window where a straight shot of scotch was served each man. Lt. Berthelsen did not drink, so he always gave me his. Then the procedure was to sit down at a table with a trained interrogator who quizzed each of us for any and all of the events that happened on the mission. The command pilot in the lead plane usually mingled with the crews at this time. Sometimes this was Col. Jimmy Stewart.

Thus our first mission was completed. That left thirty-four to go. After debriefing we went to the locker room to unload all of our flight gear. Then it was the mess hall and food. Then it was the barracks and a good night's sleep.

It was about this date that Lt. Berthelsen received a letter from his wife informing him that he was the father of a newborn son named Bryan. He came around to our hut next morning to pass out cigars.

Our next mission (#2) came on September5[th,] mission no.189 for the 389th. The routine was the same, except this time we were awakened before dawn. Another crew awakened, had in twelve missions, and we were informed by one of them that the early awakening probably meant a long mission. They were right. At briefing we learned that the target was railroad marshalling yards at Karlsruhe in southern Germany. The briefing officer informed us that at this time the Germans were withdrawing from Italy and this marshalling yard was their primary exit route. It was very important that this route be destroyed.

Our crew was assigned a war-weary spare plane. It had the old OD paint job and Consolidated hydraulic nose and tail turrets, which everyone disliked because they were about twice the discomfort as the later model Emerson electric. We took off shortly after daybreak, climbed to 10,000 feet, moved into our assigned position in the formation, and then headed south, continuing to climb enroute. When we reached the coast line, I left the waist area, climbed through the bomb-bay and carefully deposited my parachute on the forward side of the forward bulkhead. Then I proceeded to arm the bomb-load. When that was complete, I collected my chute and crawled on up to the nose compartment. I carefully stowed my chute under the turret and climbed in. Lt. Bill Faircloth closed and latched the doors behind me. This turret was designed for a five foot person. I am five foot-eight, so the fit for me was very tight.

The route to Karlsruhe was along the eastern border of France. So we did not get any flak on the way. The Swiss Alps were off in the distance. As we approached the target, Lt. Faircloth called out on the intercom, "Flak ahead" I took another look dead ahead where I see a horizontal dark line formed by 88 mm anti-aircraft shells bursting. This was not the box flak that had been described in training. These shells were all exploding at the same altitude which coincided with our formation. There is no deviation. We follow the lead plane directly into the bursts, for the Germans are placing them right over the drop zone. As we wade in, the plane starts bouncing around from the concussion of the exploding shells. Dead flak bounces off the aluminum skin like somebody throwing a hand-full of rocks. The plane ahead of us was hit in the wing fuel tanks and a stream of gasoline flowed out behind. He peeled off, left the formation, and headed for Switzerland. Spivey called on the intercom to report, "Fire in number 3 engine" Lt. Riggles hit it with the CO2 extinguisher and put it out. Somebody in the waist reported another plane in the formation had an engine fire. Then it was "bombs away." Lt. Riggles jumped on the intercom and shouted, "Let's get the hell out of here, Al," and we turned away from the turbulent mess. By this time the formation was pretty well disorganized anyway.

I was in shock. All of a sudden I realized somebody down there wanted me dead. Dead-dead! AND all I could do about it was to duck further into my flak helmet. The plexiglas turret offered no protection whatsoever. So this is war—I want no part of it! My confidence in living a long life had suddenly disappeared.

Lt. Berthelsen worked us back into the formation, and we turned north towards England. Number 3 engine was streaming black smoke. Berthelsen called to the radio operator Holdredge for help. Riggles had slumped over. Something is wrong with his oxygen supply. Holdredge crawled through the plane, collected the tiny "bail-out bottles" of oxygen, and got Riggles hooked back up. We had a two hour flight ahead of us on oxygen. Lt. Riggles would have to be very careful and connect to a fresh bottle occasionally.

The flight for the rest of the way home went ok. The number 3 engine continued to trail black smoke all the way, but it did not fail. The formation arrived back at Hethel in late afternoon. It had been a very long day. We took our turn in the landing pattern, coming in for a smooth landing. Berthelsen applied the brakes once, coasted a ways, and then hit them again. There was nothing. In the waist we noted that number 2 engine was all of a sudden engulfed in smoke. We tried to inform the cockpit of fire in number 2, but we never did raise anybody. Meanwhile the end of the runway was nearing, and we were still going at a pretty good clip. I opened the rear hatch and made ready to jump as soon as we slowed down enough. The plane came to the runway end where Berthelsen, using the right outboard engine, was able to steer around the corner onto the ramp. The 90 degree turn slowed us further, and we came to a halt. I bailed out of the rear hatch followed by the others. I was very happy to be standing on concrete. Good old mother earth!

The fire trucks arrived along with many other emergency vehicles and quite a crowd of people. I guess when they saw that cloud of smoke come out of no. 2 engine they figured we were going to need lots of help. It turned out the cloud of smoke was from hydraulic brake fluid dumped onto the red hot turbo. There was no fire. A piece of flak had nicked the brake line that leads to the left landing gear. Luckily it allowed one application of the brakes before bursting. The plane was riddled with flak holes. Again, luckily none of the crew was hit. Lt. Riggles was the only near casualty. The ground crews found his oxygen supply line cut by flak. The radio was demolished. The number 3 engine fire was caused by flak punching a hole in a valve rocker arm cover which allowed oil to leak out onto the exhaust manifold. It was fortunate that the oil supply lasted all the way back.

I went back to the barracks that night, crawled into my bunk, and was still shaking. I was scared. I said my prayers in earnest. The crew of the plane that headed for Switzerland was from our hut. In fact, it was the crew who had completed twelve missions. This had been number thirteen for them, and now they were MIA. A couple of people from headquarters came around to bag up all of their belongings, leaving six empty bunks. It was a month before we heard that they had made it to Switzerland and were now interned by the Swiss.

The second mission being completed earned us a three day pass. We chose to go to London. We talked to some of the old timers and learned where the best hotels were, where we could get some scotch, and, of course, where all of the girls hung out. WE caught a ride to Norwich where we boarded the train for the three hour trip to London.

Arriving in London about noon, we went straight to number 50 Brewers Street for the scotch. Sure enough, they had plenty--for the Americans who could pay the price. A British soldier was not even welcome in the store for their pay was a pittance. On the other hand, we were being paid pretty well with basic Sergeant scale plus 20% flight pay plus 50% combat pay. I think I was getting around $250 per month. The pay was in British pounds, so I never was sure just how much I was making, but I always had plenty for cigarettes, booze and the like. I remember sending some home for my mother to bank for me. Anyway, at this time, we took up a collection from the six of us and purchased three fifths of Black and White Scotch at $ 18.00 each. That was the black market price of the times. We went next to the hotel, I can't remember the name but it was popular for American enlisted men. We rented one big room with several beds and couches. Going upstairs, we planted our baggage and immediately opened the first bottle of scotch. This was the first booze for any of us since leaving Westover, so each of us felt it rapidly. Also, each of us felt as I did, after that mission to Karlsruhe, that this could be the last party ever. After we emptied that first bottle, we went down to the dining room for lunch. The dining room was very elegant, but all they had to serve was fish and chips. The six of us sat at a round table eating, when we were joined by an American Sailor. They were very scarce in London, out numbered by ground and air forces. Anyway this sailor had been stationed here for sometime, so he knew his way around. He joined our party to be sort of a tour guide and to share in our scotch. After the lunch was completed the seven of us went back up to the room and consumed another fifth.

By now, I was feeling no pain. I carried my Kodak and we all went downstairs and called a cab. We had all good intentions of seeing all of the famous sights of London, but we decided to go by 50 Brewers Street and replenish the scotch as it was going fast. I think we purchased two more fifths. Our first stop on the tour was Hyde Park where we rented two row-boats for the seven of us. It was a beautiful sunny day, and I was feeling very happy. The sailor and Winter were in my boat with Spivey, Holdredge, Johnson and Pounds following in their boat. We had the scotch in our boat.

Some place out in the middle of the lake, we bumped into another boat which was occupied by two Polish soldiers. Warsaw was their home, and they had escaped and joined the British Army to fight the Germans. At this period of the war, Warsaw was a no man's land, pounded by both the Germans who were moving out, and the Russians who were moving in. Anyway, we had great sympathy for these two Polish soldiers. We could not understand a word they said except that they were from Warsaw. We offered them a drink of our scotch and in passing the bottle to their boat, some how the cork was lost overboard. So we all had another drink out in the middle of the lake. I don't remember too much after that except we did make it to the far side of the lake. We sat on the grass and partied, the six of us plus the sailor and the two Poles, sort of an international party. I did take some pictures with my Kodak but not of the famous buildings of London as I had intended. Instead, I took a picture of a girl bicycling down a path that ran through the park and passed near our party spot. Also one of my buddies, with my camera, took a picture of me sitting on the grass, with my arm around this sailor. We were obviously inebriated.

I don't remember the trip back across the lake, or the taxi ride back to the hotel. But I do remember the fuss that was created when we entered the hotel lobby with these two Poles. The hotel management did not share our sympathy and wanted them out. A couple of our guys were holding them up so we took them up to our room anyway. I fell into bed and woke up the next morning feeling tough. The Poles had left. It was already time for us to catch the train back to Hethel so we packed up, checked out, and made our way to the train station. That ended our weekend pass to London.

Our next mission (#3) was on Sept. 10th, no. 192 for the 389th, to marshalling yards at the city of Ulm, in southern Germany. I don't remember any of the details. In fact, the events that took place on each mission, all run together. I can't remember what happened when. So I will list the missions by the date flown and follow with the events that stick in my mind.

Mission	Date	Target Location	Target Type	389th Mission #
# 4	Sept 11	Misburgh	O/I	#193
# 5	25	Koblenz	M/Y	#195
# 6	26	Hamm	M/Y	#199

It was about this time that our crew was assigned to our own B24, designated K+. This identified it as belonging to the 566th Squadron. Lt. Berthelsen asked all of the crew if it would be OK to have the name "LONI MAC" painted on the forward fuselage where normally some nose art would go. Loni Mac represented an abbreviation for Berthelsen's wife and Riggles girl friend. No one had any objection, thus our airplane was named after two ladies back in the states.

Lonie Mac Riggles Berthelsen Faircloth"

At about this date General Patton and his 2ⁿᵈ Army was going across France in the direction of Germany and   he started running out of gas for his tanks. The 389ᵗʰ Bomb Group was called upon to run gasoline supplies to a forward airfield in France. So our B24 was equipped with floor boards in the bomb bay and five gallon cans of gas were stacked in. We took off at around 0900 and flew at 1000 feet across the English countryside, then the channel and the coast of France. This was a very leisurely trip. We landed at this airfield which was only recently taken from the Germans. The whole crew pitched in and unloaded the gasoline cans onto the ground where ground troops took possession. Then we hitched a ride into the nearest village and went shopping. I bought a couple of bottles of French perfume to send home. (My mother and sisters went goo-goo over them I learned later). We also were treated to some of the German stocks of fancy wines which had been left behind. We traded cigarettes for wine and cognac and took the loot back to Hethel.

Earthquake McGoon Riggles & Faircloth

"Lt Faircloth in flak suit"

389th Mission number 200 called for a big celebration. The hanger was cleared out, a bandstand constructed for Glen Miller and his band. Bus loads of girls were brought in from Norwich and the surrounding country side. Jitter-bug dances were the big thing those days and there was plenty of it that night. It was a great party. It was about two weeks later that Glen Miller disappeared on a flight crossing the channel headed for Paris.

Mission,	Date ,	Target Location,	Target Type,	389th Mission #,
#7	Oct 3	Speyer	A/F	201
#8	5	Rheine	M/Y	202
#9	7	Kassel	Vehicle Factories	204
#10	12	Osnabruck	M/Y	206
#11	19	Mainz	M/Y	212
#12	22	Hamm	M/Y	214
#13	30	Hamburg		218
Lt. Harvey Muskrat, navigator assigned to our crew				
#14	Nov 2	Bielefeld	M/Y	220
#15	9	Metz, France	T/T	224

#16	10	Hanau	M/Y	225
#17	21	Hamburg	M/Y	227
#18	30	Homburg	M/Y	232
#19	Dec 2	Bingen	M/Y	233
#20	11	Maxmiliansau	R/B	238
#21	12	Hanau	M/Y	240

On another mission, an event that I witnessed from that nose turret was one of Von Braun's V2 rockets going up to near orbit. Our formation was out over the North Sea, flying east and paralleling the Netherlands coast. We were at 25,000 feet, which was about as high as anything went in those days. Off in the distance at about 2 o'clock I see this vehicle trailing smoke and headed for the heavens.. It looked to be the size of a box car. It went up and up until it was out of sight, eventually to come down on London. It was very impressive. I was witness to the beginnings of the Space Age.

Another nasty event that I saw was on one cloudless day in October when the formation was crossing over Belgium headed into Germany. The terrain below was forest covered hills. The navigator called on the intercom and as a matter of interest said we were now crossing the Siegfried line. I was watching a formation of B24's flying parallel to us about a mile away, apparently headed for the same target. The Germans must have had their best anti-aircraft gunners down there defending that Siegfried line as one four gun battery started following that formation with 88 bursts, each burst closer to tail end Charlie. The fourth shell nailed the wing of one of the rear B24's. It went down like a rock, in flames, tumbling end over end. I could almost feel the whole crew being roasted alive at 20,000 feet. There were no parachutes.

The fighter escort on our early missions was mixed. Sometimes we had P38's, sometimes P47's and sometimes P51's. The P51's were the best because with their fifty gallon drop tanks, they could go almost the distance as the bombers. But there were not enough of them to go around at this time, so we had to settle for whatever was available. One clear day in October we had P47's. They called this fighter "the Jug" because of its blunt nose and short stubby wings. It was fast. It was rumored that if one of them got on a Germans tail in a dive, the P47 did not have to fire a shot to finish the German. From my nose turret I witnessed this exact scene. An ME110 twin engine German fighter passed straight in front of my turret, headed for the ground with a P47 right on his tail. The ME110, in trying to escape the P47, got going so fast in the dive, he could not pull up.

The P47, with its stubby wings had no trouble pulling out, thus he made a kill without firing a shot.

Beginning in late October, the weather became a real hazard. The weather over the target area was the all important factor. On some missions we were obliged to take off and form up in cloud cover up to 10-12,000 feet. There was strict radio silence, no ground control, no nothing except pilots were instructed to keep in a counterclockwise circle around a radio beacon sent up for radio compass use.

" SSgt's Bill Crum & Willie Pounds"

"SSgt Bill Crum & CO's P47"

On October 30th, on a mission to Hamburg, somewhere over Germany on the way to the target, the cloud cover came up to meet us. The weather forecasters had goofed in predicting the weather at the target. Here is the whole 389th group, about 48 B24's, flying wing tip to wing tip and suddenly engulfed in fog like clouds. From my turret, I could not see the lead plane. The formation held together by following the plane in front of your own. We reached the target and bombed using radar. On another mission, the formation was pushing the altitude limit of the B24's when we flew into a sever weather front. All of a sudden there is Zero visibility. This caused the group to disperse in a pre-arranged fashion and pray that it works. Our plane peeled off to the left and down. About two minutes went by when we slammed into an ice cloud. In seconds my plexi-glass was covered with ice. It hit so hard I thought it would come through. The pilot and co-pilot were conversing about the wing de-icer. They must have worked for in a few minutes we leveled out and were flying just below the surface of the clouds. I could look straight up and see patches of clear blue sky. About this time, Spivey in the upper turret saw 20 mm cannon shells flashing over the right wing. Apparently, some smart ass German was taking advantage of all the cloud cover and was sitting just above shooting down at us. Fortunately, he missed.

"Tail Gunners View" here

"Pilots Side Window View"

One day in early November, a few weeks after Paris had been liberated. I was standing in the chow line at Hethel and was dumbfounded to meet my old friend Bill Hennes. He was from Southern California. He was drafted at the same time as I was. We went through basic at Kearns, then on to Lowery for Armament together. We parted company when I took time out for my sister's death. But we were at Lowery together in the beginning and long enough for me to introduce him to Dotty one night in Denver. I had encountered him again at Westover, also while waiting in the chow line. It seemed like I was following him around the US, and now he turns up at Hethel. Only this time Bill did not look so good. In fact he did not talk so good. He was stuttering when telling me about being shot down on his 12th mission, in flames while bombing from 12,000 feet, the German front lines at St. Lo in France. He had baled out of his burning B24 and landed on the German side, pretty well roasted. He was put into an ambulance along with several bloodied Germans. They took off down the road away from the target area. The ambulance was stalked by a P51 and I guess Bill and the Germans were praying that the P51 pilot would honor the Red Cross painted on top of the vehicle. He did.   Bill landed in a hospital in Paris as a POW where he was being treated for his burns. One day the Germans just up and left, leaving him and the other patients in their beds. Paris had been liberated. Soon he was returned to Hethel. I never saw him again after this meeting in the chow line. I'm sure his combat days were over, and he was probably returned to stateside.

I wrote Dottie about Bill's experience. Since I did not mention his name, I did not believe any classified information was included. I identified him in the letter as the fellow that we met in Denver one night. I mailed the letter off to Dottie. A week later I was called on the carpet--to the squadron commander's office. Standing in front of his desk, he proceeded to show me this letter that had come back from the censor in London. So much of the letter had been censored that the sheet of paper was mostly holes. The Colonel reamed me out good for mentioning in the mail anything about an escaped POW. Also, since some officers initials were on the envelope as indicating the letter had been censored before leaving Hethel, they figured that I had forged the initials. I told him that I had no reason to forge the censor's initials because I did not know I was giving away any classified information. The Colonel accepted that answer and said, "If anybody asks you, you are restricted to the base for two weeks." He kept my chopped up letter, and I suppose he went after the officer who initialed the envelope.

On yet another mission, I was a near casualty out the open bomb bay doors over the North Sea. Our bomb load on this mission was incendiary's. The bomb on the bottom is about two feet in diameter and is supposed to drop first. Above it, on each of the other five release mechanisms, were small one hundred pounders strapped three together so that each of the four vertical racks had one incendiary on the bottom release and fifteen one hundred pound bombs above. The idea was the phosphorus incendiary landed on the target, then all of the fifteen ordinary bombs, come down and scatter the burning phosphorus. That's the way it is supposed to work. But on this mission, a malfunction occurred on the forward left rack. When the bombs were released over the target, the incendiary hung up so did not drop. The fifteen armed bombs above it were released normally and lodged between the incendiary and the side of the fuselage. We left the target and flew in the formation back to the North Sea. Lt. Berthelsen radioed to the lead plane that we had a problem in the bomb bay and would leave the formation, dropping down to 5000 feet. We had to get rid of those loose bombs before arriving over England. So when the time came, I left my nose turret, crawled back to the bomb bay. I was shocked at the tangle of live bombs. Several of the 100 pounders were only inches away from the control cables running along the fuselage. Since this problem fell in my area of responsibility, I told the bombardier my plan. I would straddle the open bomb bay and try to push the bombs forward and out one at a time. I did not want them to go all at once because they were fully armed. If they bumped together when falling, there might be an explosion which could be hazardous to our B24. So here I am, supporting myself with my left foot on the side of the fuselage and my right foot on the catwalk. I grabbed the first bomb by the tail fin, trying to lift and push it forward far enough to tip it over and out. I soon had to give that up as it was too heavy for the awkward position from which I was lifting. I had just let go of that tail fin when zip, the bottom incendiary released and the whole mess exited the plane, leaving me staring at the ocean 5,000 feet below. I had not noticed that the radio operator, Holdredge, was squatted down on the catwalk and was prying on the bottom bomb release with a screw driver. He succeeded in making it work, but I hate to think of my fate had I not let go of that 100 pound tail fin when I did. Also, the bombs did not bump together and explode. My guardian angel was busy this day!

On a mission to Hanau, 12th December, a number of errors took place costing the lives of ten men and a B24. We were on the bomb run when the formation hit turbulence, which caused some near collisions. The B24 flying off our wing had to dive under our plane in order to avoid taking our tail off. For some yet unexplained reason, the deputy lead dropped his bombs early. I jumped the gun and called out "bombs away" when I saw those bombs falling. The bombardier took my word for it and released our bomb-load. A moment later, our B24 was lifted up from a terrific explosion directly under us. The tail gunner called on the intercom and said that the largest piece of that aircraft left was the box of flares that are carried on the flight deck. They had been ignited and were making like a 4th of July display. A moment later, the lead plane dropped and the rest of the formation--except us--dropped co-incidentally. On our return to Hethel, the camera from our plane was rushed to the lab for development of the strike photos. The photos were not shown to us, but the bombardier, Lt. Bill Faircloth came back to us with the word that the developed pictures had shown a B24 with a wing crumbling and the inboard engine missing. In other words, the B24 that exploded while under us had taken a direct hit from an 88 shell and not one of our bombs. I chose to believe the story but doubts have remained with me.

Missions were interrupted at this time for ten days R and R (rest and recuperation) in the Flak home which was located in the south west of England, a two day train ride with overnight stop in London. The rest home was operated jointly by the Air Force and the Red Cross. It was a wealthy old estate, even had its own golf course. On arrival there, we were met by a Red Cross girl, assigned to a bed in an upstairs bed room, issued civilian clothes which was quite a surprise, especially when told that we could wear them into the nearby town. We were treated like royalty, fresh orange juice served in bed. GREAT. Breakfast, lunch and dinner served in a dining room. There were bicycles to ride into town to visit the local pubs, skeet shooting and use of the golf course. It was a very pleasant week.

"R&R Skeet Shooting" here

We returned to Hethel on December 24th, Christmas Eve. This was very lucky timing as we missed out on a maximum effort, 2000 plane mission flown on Christmas Day. This was in support of our ground forces in the "Battle of the Bulge." The Germans were making a last all out effort and the 389th was hit by fighters, losing three B24s.

We resumed flying a few days after Christmas as follows:

Mission,	Date,	Target Location,	Target Type,	389th Mission #
#22	Dec 27	Kaiserslautern	M/Y	246
#23	29	Fensbach		248
#24	30	Auskirchen	R/B	253
#25	31	Koblenz	R/B	250
	1945			
#26	Jan 3	Homburg	M/Y	253
#27	6	Bonn Rhine	H/B	256
#28	7	Zweibrucken	M/Y	257

#29	14	Ehmen	O/I	259
#30	16	Magdeburg	M/I	260
#31	28	Dortmund	O/I	262

H/B = high way bridge   O/I = oil installation

R/B = rail road bridge   A/F = air field

M/Y = marshalling yards   T/T = tactical target

A weather-related problem occurred one day in January when in returning to base we found cloud cover hugging the ground. We prowled around at tree top level for the better part of an hour, with flaps and landing gear lowered, looking for any landing strip. I stood at the waist window looking down into the farmyards. I could count the chickens in the pen. Very hazardous as many other B24's were cruising around in those clouds with the same problem. Also, there was wind-shear activity. We hit an up draft that elevated us 500 feet. Lt. Berthelsen let loose with some choice words. The plane remained in level flight, but it gained 500 feet like it was riding a fast elevator, and he had no control of it. Finally an air strip was sighted in time to line up and set down. It was an adjacent field to Hethel so after the landing we were trucked back. Somebody picked up our plane, returning it to Hethel the next day.

"Returning to Hethel from a mission"

So it went. Some missions went without a hitch. After # 30, I began to have hopes of going home. In fact, I made the mistake of writing my mother that I might make it home for my birthday. Instead, she received a telegram from the War department that her son, Staff Sgt. Willard L. Crum was missing in action- MIA as of January 28th. Another mistake, I went ahead and decorated my A2 leather jacket with thirty-five bombs, indicating thirty-five missions accomplished. T/Sgt. Spivey, being somewhat superstitious, said this was bad medicine. God rest his soul. I wish I had listened to him. This was a big, big lesson in "NEVER COUNT YOUR CHICKENS BEFORE THEY HATCH."

CHAPTER VI

EXPENDED
OR
MY LONGEST DAY

The day began with the before dawn wake-up call. The duty sergeant wanders through the Quonset hut and locates each crewmember by the name tag on the foot of each bunk, grabs a foot and shakes each awake, then moves on to find the next man on his list. He works very quietly and uses a flashlight so as not to disturb those lucky fellows not assigned to fly this day. They get to sleep in, in their nice warm bed. The date was Sunday, January 28, 1945. The temperature, once out of the bedcovers, was about twenty degrees, so no time is wasted getting into several layers of clothing.

This was to be mission number thirty-one for our crew, with only four more to go. At this time in the air war over Europe, the heavy bomber crew's tour of duty was thirty-five missions. After making it through thirty, some easy and some horrible, I was beginning to feel that I would maybe survive. I was nose turret gunner on the B24 Liberator crew of Lt. Al Berthelsen, and from that Plexiglas enclosure I had already seen enough violence to last me a lifetime. It was easy to die 25,000 ft. over Germany. If not from ME109s or those nasty 88 mm antiaircraft guns on the ground, it was from collisions with the wingman, a loose 50 caliber machine gun somewhere in the formation or something simple like becoming disconnected from your oxygen supply. Another hazard was frostbite, as Winter temperatures at those altitudes were often 30 or 40 degrees below F. Anyway, I had the most viewing area on the airplane as I could see in all directions except straight behind and straight below. Some of the things I saw out of that nose I can still see today--50 years later.

Our assigned aircraft was a brand new J model. It was designated K+ and we had named it "Lonie Mac", derived from the pilot and copilot's wives' names. Our crew consisted of ten men, as follows:

1st Lt	Alvin L. Berthelsen	Pilot	Omaha, Nebraska
2nd Lt	Thomas Riggles	Copilot	Middle River, Maryland
2nd Lt.	Harvey R. Muskrat	Navigator	Stewart, Nevada
*2nd Lt	William T. Faircloth	Bombardier	New Orleans, Louisiana

T/Sgt.	Keith M Holdredge	Radio Operator	McDonough, New York
*T/Sgt.	Charles H. Spivey	Engineer/Top turret	Mystic, Georgia
S/Sgt.	Willard L. Crum	Armorer/Nose turret	Van Nuys, California
*S/Sgt.	Donald G. Johnson	Waist Gunner	Minn., Minnesota
*S/Sgt.	Willie G. Pounds	Waist Gunner	Birmingham, Alabama
S/Sgt.	Louis V. Winter	Tail Gunner	Lulu, Mississippi

*MIA/ KIA

Except for Muskrat, the navigator, and Faircloth the bombardier, we trained together at Westover Field, Mass., flew the Atlantic in July in a brand new B24 bomber and subsequently were assigned to the 566th Squadron, 389th Bomb Group, 2nd Air Division of the 8th Army Air Force.

Our air station was an ex-RAF base adjacent to the tiny village of Hethel, Norfolk County, on the southeast coast of England. This day we would be flying a spare airplane because our own was out of commission. We had been forced to abandon it at an airfield in France on the previous mission due to number 3 engine blown. So today we would be flying a different B24, Miss America C+. This aircraft was equipped with some super secret radar, which turned out to be an early version of radar counter measures. All that we were told was that the equipment occupied space on the flight deck, and it required an operator. Hence, for this mission, we had an 11 man crew. T/Sgt. Phillip G. DeFalco was the radar man.

"Miss America"

Breakfast and briefing went as usual. At briefing we learned the target was to be synthetic fuel plants at the city of Dortmund in the Ruhr Valley of Germany. The route was to be across the North Sea, across Holland into Germany, turning south-east to the target, continuing in the same direction after the target, and then circling back over Holland and then the North Sea. We would be only an hour over enemy territory and the route was chosen for minimum flak, we were told at briefing.

After briefing comes the short walk to the locker room to suit up: electric heated suit, maewest, oxygen mask, helmet, fur-lined boots, parachute and a 45 automatic pistol in a shoulder holster. I would guess about twenty pounds are added to the person's weight with all of this equipment but the only option was the 45 automatic. I chose not to carry one because I figured it would only get me into trouble. The oxygen mask is life itself at the altitude at which we flew while over enemy territory. Once airborne, there was no turning back for any unfortunate crewman who was careless enough to leave his behind. The maewest was AAF regulation any time flying over water but in our case was probably a waste of time because if you were unfortunate enough to come down in the North Sea, the water temperature would do you in before you could drown. The parachute was something you hoped you would never need, but let me assure you, after the shooting starts on the very first trip anywhere over Germany, that parachute was a mighty precious piece of equipment and it was given a lot of tender loving care. I was very happy, when in December the nose and tail turret gunners were issued backpack-type chutes which could be worn inside the turret. Before this, we had a chest type which had to be stowed outside the turret, and sometimes due to the accuracy of the German's firepower, a turret got separated from the rest of the airplane.

After suiting up and gathering all flight equipment, it is outside where the crew gathers together, climbs aboard a GI 6x6 truck and rides out into the woods where C+ is parked on its respective hardstand. It was still dark out, but everything was right on schedule up to this point. We reached the aircraft, climbed down out of the truck, and were greeted by the crew chief. Our pilot had a few words with him and was assured that the ship was all set to go; 2,500 gallons of 120 octane gasoline, 8,000 lbs. bomb-load, 500 rounds of 50 caliber ammunition for each of the ten machine guns, flak suits, etc. All added up, the airplane had to be grossly overloaded. It is a tribute to the design that it could get off the ground.

We climbed aboard, each man taking his turn to enter through the open bomb bay doors. The pilot, copilot, navigator, bombardier, radio operator, engineer/top turret gunner and radar operator all went forward to the flight deck while the two waist gunners, the tail gunner and I went to the rear section of the aircraft. This was the regular routine, and this is where we would stay until after takeoff. So now the idea is to make yourself as comfortable as possible to wait for daylight and the signal to start engines.

This is no easy problem as the only seats in the aircraft were for the pilot and copilot. The rest of us had to hunker down and try to keep warm the best we could. The cold was a big problem. This day the temperature, both inside and out, was around ZERO degrees, and until engine start there is no power available for the electric heated clothing.

Daylight finally started to arrive but still no signal to start engines. The word was passed that there was ice on the runway along with every place else. This was the coldest day ever this Winter which made for dangerous takeoffs. Maybe the mission would be scrubbed, we hoped. An hour went by, and the dawn changed to a cold stormy Winter morning. There was still no word to go. I decided I needed a BM. As much as I hated the idea, I climbed down out the bomb bay, walked through the snow and into the woods a very short distance, found a log to hang my rear over, undid all the drawers I was wearing, and had my BM. I pulled back on all the clothing, rebuckeled on my chute and made my way back to the ship. Shortly thereafter the word came over the intercom from the pilot that we were going, and simultaneously he started cranking up number one engine, then number two, three and four. We moved off the hardstand out onto the perimeter taxi strip and on out to the lineup of bombers at the end of the north/south runway. Once out in the open, it was obvious that the weather was terrible, just short of a blizzard. In spite of that we took our position in the line, and when our turn came we turned onto the runway and took off. After climbing up through 12,000 ft. of clouds, there was the sun, beautiful as ever. During the Winter months in England, one could forget what the sun looked like. That was one part of the mission that I always enjoyed, climbing up through the clouds to meet the sun, like a submarine surfacing in the middle of the ocean. There were other reasons to rejoice when breaking through the clouds. There was always a few hundred other bombers up there circling and climbing, circling and climbing. In those days, it took a couple of hours for a fully loaded bomber to climb to 15,000 ft. If any one ship strayed out of his prescribed territory, look out. There were many collisions during the Winter of 1944-45. This meant two aircraft and twenty men lost, plus maybe citizen casualties on the ground.

We finally arrived at our prearranged altitude, located the rest of our group, and took our position in the formation. The formation circled a couple more times to pick up all the latecomers, and then we headed out over the North Sea. Now it was time for me to go to work. Being the armament specialist of the crew, it was my job to climb through the bomb bay and arm the bombs by pulling the safety pins on each bomb. The rule was this was to be done after leaving the coast of England. I informed the pilot that I was about to begin this activity and started through the bulkhead door and onto the catwalk. The bomb load was 500 pounders, five on each rack, and four racks. This was a very awkward job what with all the bulky clothing, maewest and parachute. It was a tight fit to walk the cat walk between the upright bomb rack, stoop over and work on the lower bombs. I had to work with gloves on because if I took them off and touched any part of the airplane, there was almost instant frost bite. And one couldn't linger too long on this job because at 15,000 ft. a person could run out of oxygen and pass out.

This day I got all of the bombs armed. Then I continued through the forward bulkhead, crawled through the tunnel under the flight deck, past the nose wheel and into the navigator/bombardier compartment. Lt. Harvey Muskrat and Lt. Bill Faircloth were already at work at their station. I opened the doors to the nose turret and pulled myself up and into the turret feet first via a chinning maneuver. Then Lt. Muskrat closed and latched the doors behind me. I plugged in my headset, my oxygen hose, and power to my electric suit. Soon the word comes over the headset for all gun positions to test fire the guns. Just be careful of the plane flying alongside and our own plane for that matter. From the waist positions it was possible to shoot up your own ship. From the nose turret, I could fire from 3 o'clock to 9 o'clock and up and down from the horizontal about 70 degrees. I aimed my guns down toward the North Sea and pulled the trigger for a short blast. Everything is OK. Now I am ready for business and inform the pilot as such.

It is lonely up here. I am almost surrounded by Plexiglas, except for the doors at my back and the seat underneath. Yet I am isolated from everybody else in the aircraft except by the intercom. So I like to talk, keep in touch with the rest of the crew. Sometimes this got me in trouble. When the shooting started I would get uptight and start swearing at the Krauts and relaying everything I saw going on. This didn't go over too well with some of the crew. They would rather not know of all the nasty business going on up ahead.

The flight across the North Sea went without problem. Then we crossed the coastline of Holland and headed toward the IP. No opposition so far. It did not take very long to reach the IP, which was right on the Holland/German border. We turned southeast at the IP and shortly thereafter opened the bomb bay doors. This is the sign for the Germans to start shooting in earnest if they haven't already. By whatever means, with their binoculars, when they see those bomb bays open, they decide very quickly what the target is to be and a black cloud soon forms over that exact bomb release point, and we are committed to fly straight into it. The bombardier in the lead plane has the target lined up in his bombsight, and there is no dodging of flak bursts or anything else. During this critical period, the whole effort is focused on hitting the target. If it is missed, the whole mission has been wasted.

The German anti aircraft gunners with their 88s do their best to knock out the lead plane, but it seems like they don't care which plane because over the target they just pour it on. There are 88s bursting every place you look. You hear WHUMPH--and feel the ship rock with the concussion. You know that one was too close. WHUMPH again and this time the 88 went off 50 ft. above, and an instant later it sounds like somebody threw a handful of rocks at the plane as the dead flak bounces off the aluminum skin. Finally the lead plane drops the bomb load which is the signal for the rest of the twelve plane formation to drop. The bombardier has his eyes glued to the lead ship and sounds "bombs away!" The B24 jumps when the bomb load goes. The bomb bay doors are closed and now the focus is on getting back to Hethel. The pilot takes roll call over the intercom to make sure we are all still with him. This mission everybody answers.

Heading off of the target is the time to watch for the Luftwaffe, for they would wait on the far side of the target for two reasons: first, they were not foolish enough to fly into the clouds of flak; second, it was easy pickings of any poor bomber which lagged behind or got separated from the formation by the flak. No Luftwaffe today as we continue on course down the Ruhr. The 88 gunners are tracking us now. There are not a lot of bursts, but what there are follows us, some above, some below, some out in front, and even though I could not see them from my nose turret, I know there were some out behind us. The radar counter measure equipment did not seem to be working too well. This was not surprising. We were bombing visually, so I'm sure the gunners on the ground could use their visual sight to aim at us.

The time was about 12 noon, and we were about five minutes past the target. The navigator called on the intercom to inform us that we would soon be out of the Ruhr and the heavy flak area. He also mentioned as a matter of interest that the temperature was -55 degrees, the coldest we had ever experienced in our thirty missions.

WHOOMPH--that was a close one. Then out of the corner of my eye I saw an 88 shell streak upward about ten ft. out in the 9 o'clock position, and then burst about 100 ft. above us. An instant later WHOOMPH--the left wing was lifted way up to approximately 45 degrees. Then it dropped back down towards the horizontal--but did not stop. The next thing I knew, I was staring at the ground, and it was going round and round straight out in front of my nose turret. Nobody needed to tell me that it was time to make a fast exit from that turret and part company with this aircraft. I jerked on my door release handle, and the doors opened behind me. I took a quick glance behind me and observed Lts Muskrat and Faircloth were already bent down over the nose wheel doors. They were in the process of pulling the red handle that releases the two doors out into space and leaves a nice big exit hole in the bottom of the nose compartment.

My next move was to jerk free of all the wires and hoses that attached me to that doomed B24. This was mostly accomplished by peeling my leather helmet off. Next move was to lift myself backward out of that turret requiring sort of a reverse chinning exercise. I grabbed the handles above and behind my head and was surprised at how fast I elevated myself out of there. The B24 rate of descent provided me with almost zero gravity. In fact I came out so fast I left my boots, socks and all, in the turret, and I didn't slow down to retrieve them. Once out of the turret, I took note that Lts Muskrat and Faircloth were already gone out the now open hatch.

It was chaos in the compartment. The navigator's maps and papers were flying around in a circle, caught like in a whirlwind. The lid on the right hand storage box of 50 caliber ammunition had come off, and the belt of 50's was suspended in mid-air, similar to a snake dancing. I was about to take the few steps to the open hatch when the nose wheel began to descend, just as if we were going in for a normal landing. This presented me with an unexpected obstacle. I dared not try to beat the wheel out the exit for I could be caught and crushed between the wheel and the frame of the opening. I must have spent a precious second debating if I should crawl back through the tunnel and exit via the bomb bay. This was not a good idea because the plane's angle of descent made that tunnel a long climb, and I would probably run out of oxygen and become unconscious before reaching the bomb bay. So I waited the few seconds that it took the nose wheel to reach the extended position. Then I had a new problem. The wheel strut, centered in the middle of the hole, blocked my exit. I made another quick survey and decided that to the rear of the strut was the largest opening. So I took the few steps around the nose wheel to the rear, knelt down facing forward and stuck my head down to the opening, trying to decide if I would fit. Now with my head down near the open exit I can hear the propellers chopping away at the air, and now I had a new concern. Would I clear those deadly props once out into the slipstream? A horrible thought if I didn't! I stuck my head a little further out to determine if I would miss the props--whoosh--I was caught by the vacuum created by the slipstream, and I was sucked out like a straw in the wind.

I never touched the airplane. I came out tumbling over and over. I was aware of seeing the bottom of the ship go by, a view that I had never seen since training days riding in the ball turret. I held my breath, waiting to land in those props, but it never happened. A few seconds went by and I realized that I was clear of that beast. My body straightened out and I found myself falling face up. The rest of the formation--now one short--was continuing on course, homeward bound, back to Hethel and that nice warm sack. I suddenly felt very lonely and aware of being left behind to a very uncertain future, if any future at all. I had been expended!!

Soon the B24 formation was out of sight. The 88 gunners on the ground gave up on them, and it grew very quiet. I began to think about opening my chute. Since it was a backpack and inaccessible to open by hand, I wanted plenty of altitude left to fight with it if it did not open via the release cable attached to the left shoulder. I waited a short additional time, keeping in mind our training instruction which said to wait until you see the ground coming up at you before pulling the rip cord. I grasped the cable handle in my right hand and decided to wait no longer. I pulled hard. Oh man--just what I was afraid of!! The handle, cable and all came off in my hand. I looked at it, then threw it away and was surprised to see it seemingly float away, falling towards earth only a little faster than myself. I was debating what to do next, when BAM the chute opened with a mighty jerk on my crotch, and I found myself floating down at normal parachute rate.

I immediately started looking around for other chutes. I spotted two open chutes above me, but they were too far away to see who it was. I assumed it to be Muskrat and Faircloth, since they were out of the plane just ahead of me. I tried shouting at them, but to my surprise, the shout didn't seem to go anyplace. I suddenly became aware of the death-like silence. Four miles up here in semi-space, the acoustics are very dead. How weird. I gave up shouting and looked around for other chutes. Straight below me I spotted our B24, still spinning towards the earth. The left wing was missing from the no. 1 engine out. There was no fire which was very unusual because the wing carries all thousand gallons of 120 octane fuel. Somehow, an 88 explosion had cut the wing off between fuel cells.

I glued my eyes on that broken B24, praying for more chutes to come out. I don't know if my eyeballs were frozen or the snow-covered ground concealed the white chutes. I couldn't detect any more chutes. As I watched the B24 plow into the snow and disintegrate into a mass of flames, I thought that the three of us in the nose compartment were the only ones to have escaped.

It was while staring at that burning mass 18,000 ft. straight below that I noticed my bare feet hanging out. They were already turning purple. Then I remembered leaving my boots in the nose turret. Now what do I do to save my feet? Suspended in a parachute harness the feet cannot be reached. About this time I discovered I was still clutching my leather helmet in my left hand, so I dangled it down as far as

I could in an attempt to cover my feet bottoms from the wind chill factor created by my descent. I managed to get the helmet under both feet with one of the straps between my ankles for support, but I couldn't hold it for long. It soon dropped away. Well, I did the best I could. If I was to lose my feet, there was nothing I could do to prevent it until I got to the ground--which was still about 15,000 ft down. That figures out to approximately fifteen minutes, which now makes me sorry that I opened my chute so soon. Another aspect to the same mistake was the miles of drift. At approximately 10,000 ft., I began to take note of the countryside below. I was apparently drifting in a southeasterly direction and was several miles from where I started because the burning B24 was no longer in sight, nor any other parachutes. There were a few small villages discernible, but mostly just snow covered earth with a few clumps of trees scattered about. It looked about as inviting as the middle of the Pacific Ocean, and it would soon be me and only me, against whatever was left of the German nation.

As I descended closer to the dear old fatherland, I noticed all the antiaircraft batteries scattered around. They looked like little circles in the snow with the gun mechanism in the center. There was a railroad and power lines in the distance but getting closer. Now my angle of drift looks like I might be carried into those power lines. I tried pulling on my shroud lines to steer me the other direction, but I gave that up very quickly for fear of collapsing the whole chute. Anyway, as I get closer I can see that I will clear by at least a couple of hundred feet. Now I see some soldiers come out of a nearby gun emplacement and start through the snow towards my projected impact point. There were three of them, helmets, long overcoats and rifles. The ground comes up very fast now, and before I know it I am sitting in about two feet of snow. The Germans were still a couple hundred yards away, so I ignored them and began rubbing my purple feet. They looked bad, and I was far more worried about them than of the approaching Germans.

The three of them arrived, all out of breath, but all three had their rifles pointed at me. As soon as they had me encircled, the leader motioned for me to stand up. That ended the foot care. I got to my feet, and the one in front of me immediately started frisking me, while one behind kept a rifle jabbed in my back. The frisking was first, going through my pockets, and everything he found went into his pockets. The big prize seemed to be my escape kit (so-called). It contained some French money, a detailed beautiful map printed on silk, vitamin pills, etc. He was disappointed in my wrist watch, for I was wearing a $5 Westclox that I had bought some years before when I worked at Mid City Drug store back home. I was getting on to these guys fast, souvenir hunting was first priority. All three of them looked like they were only about sixteen years old.

My first priority was my feet, but I stood there with my hands high while they fooled around searching me. One was asking me "Pistolet--Pistolet???" and I kept shaking my head NO. I wasn't carrying the 45 in a shoulder holster issued to all 8th AAF crews. The German kid didn't believe me, and proceeded to continue the search where he knew the shoulder holster should be, which was underneath my parachute chest strap, and he was having trouble getting the big steel buckle undone. So of all this time I am only worried about my feet, standing on first one foot, then the other. I unconsciously decided to help with that steel buckle, hoping to speed things up so I could get back to attending my feet. This was a BIG mistake!!! As soon as I took my hands down to help with the chest buckle--WHAM--I felt a rifle jam into my back, and I reached for the sky again. These kids were not to be fooled with. The one in front finally got inside all my clothing and was satisfied that I carried no "Pistolet." I think they were disappointed.

After the search was completed, I got to sit down and continue attending to my feet. By this time there is a nice little circle of packed-down snow with the four of us in the middle and my collapsed chute off to one side. Then the three Germans became excited and started pointing at the sky. There was another bomber formation coming our way. I didn't see anything to get excited about, as I knew there was no target within miles of this place. But the Germans kept on pointing at the sky, and then one of them pointed at my silk chute lying in the snow. Me--I'm still only worried about my feet, so I imagined them using the chute for a sling and carrying me through the snow to wherever they were so suddenly in such a hurry to get to. I took the few steps and stood in the middle of it. WRONG again. I'm sure I was called several names and given a shove off the chute. Then the chute was gathered up by one of them and shoved at me. The four of us took off on a run through the snow, single file towards a railroad trestle a hundred yards away. We barely arrived at the wooden railroad trestle and down the bank to the underside when the 88 gun batteries started working on this new B24 formation that by now was almost directly overhead. My captors lead me under the trestle to where a group of civilians was also taking shelter--not from the bombers I learned, but from the dead flak that they knew would come raining down. And sure enough, as the B24 formation came overhead, the nearby gun batteries were busy. What a horrible battle noise those 88s made. With the drone of the bombers overhead, it was deafening. Then the dead flak started raining down. A heavy CLUNK was heard each time a chunk hit the wooden trestle. This stuff was as deadly on the ground as it was five miles up in the sky.

While all this was going on, I had sat down and begun rubbing my feet. The civilians gathered around, and I became the main topic of conversation. The women were admiring the silk material of my parachute, while at the same time scowling at me. A pretty girl about twelve years old with blue eyes and long blonde pigtails sat down opposite me and started massaging my feet with snow. I was more than grateful, but it didn't last long because big mama woke up to what her little girl was doing, grabbed her by the collar, yanking her to her feet at the same time scolding her good. The little girl got her first lesson in hating the enemy. I was a "Chicago Gungster" and not deserving of being treated as another human being. I could not understand a word being said except "Chicago gangster," but I sure got the message anyway. I had to feel sorry for the little girl. She looked so surprised to learn that this young man was to be hated instead of helped.

Soon the bombers had passed, and the 88s gunners gradually gave up, indicated by the diminishing thunder of their guns. All grew quiet and now my three captors began debating as to what they were supposed to do with me. Eventually the leader motioned for me to follow him and the other two fell in behind me single file. We climbed the embankment which supported the trestle, and walked a hundred yards down the tracks to a train depot. There was a train sitting there, apparently waiting for the bomber activity to be over. The leader of our little group climbed the steps up into the rear car, and I followed. I must have been getting some feeling back in my feet, for climbing the steep steps, then walking down the aisle to a bench where the leader told me to sit, felt like I was walking on frozen glass. The car was unheated and the floor might as well have been made of ice. How was I supposed to keep my bare feet off of it?

I suspect my three youthful captors were enjoying this new duty as they were getting lots of attention from the civilians. Obviously they didn't catch one of us bad guys every day. A well-dressed civilian gentleman, probably in his forties, came down the aisle, stopped in front of me and asked in perfect English, "Where are you from?" I answered California. He said, "My home is Seattle, Washington. Don't worry. These guys won't hurt you." At this point my captors told the English speaking civilian to be on his way. It was against the rules to communicate with their prisoner--unless it was swearing and name-calling.

Taking note of my surroundings, the majority of people in the station and on the train were women and children. There were a few men in uniform, older and some walking wounded. The train and station house seemed to be in great shape with the exception of no heat. Everybody was bundled up in their winter overcoats and headgear. This place was obviously out in the country, and there were no signs of bomb damage. Even so, I noticed that everybody that came down the aisle to get a look at me had a big frown on their face and most had something nasty to say--I don't know what, but I got the message just the same.

Soon the train conductor came by collecting tickets. He took one look at our four man party and went on down the aisle. The train started up and headed down the tracks in a southwesterly direction. We must have traveled for about an hour at full speed. We came to a fair sized city the name of which I do not know. I followed the leader down the aisle and off the train. We walked, single file, through the city's frozen streets, me in my bare feet.

Eventually, we came to an office in a building that turned out to be the local Luftwaffe headquarters. We entered the building, and then moved into a large room. There were several Luftwaffe personnel present in the room. Then the captain came in, and there was much clicking of heels and HEIL HITLERS. This was an older, gray-haired gent who made it clear he wasn't happy about me interrupting his Sunday afternoon social life. He paced back and forth in front of me, calling me all sorts of names. I could only sit there and look dumb, for try as I might, I could not catch a word he said. From his gestures, scowl, and tone I sure got the message. Part of the problem was that the dumb Werhmact 88 gunners had brought me to the wrong place, and now this office was stuck with me--on a Sunday afternoon. The captain soon calmed down and started giving out orders to his people. He dismissed the three 88 gunners with a growl. I realized then that I was in custody of the Luftwaffe for which I was grateful.

A half hour went by. I think a few phone calls were made concerning my disposition. Also, a young lady appeared on the scene to look at my feet. She took one look, disappeared for a couple of minutes, and returned with some warm soaked towels wrapping one around each foot. I didn't feel much difference for a few minutes, but gradually some feeling came back. The woman left the room again, and this time she came back with a pair of leather open toe sandals. They were anything but Winter type shoes, but at least there were leather soles to insulate my feet bottoms from the frozen walks. I thanked the lady and proceeded to try them on.

By this time the captain was briefing two men on what-when-how was to be done with me. I could tell this because he was pointing, looking at the wall clock and making all kinds of motions that meant travel. Subsequently

I learned that the rules stated that all bomber crews parachuting into Germany are to be taken to the Luftwaffe base nearest to their target, and there to be assembled with other crew members and participants of that raid. The 88 gun crew, still wet behind the ears, had put me on the train headed away from the target city of Dortmund, so now I must be close to a hundred miles southwest of where I should have been taken. No wonder the captain was upset, for as I soon learned, there was no transportation other than trains, and they were fast becoming very dangerous, what with all the bombing and strafing. From what I saw, the home front was totally dependent on the trains for transportation. In the city everybody walked. So when I departed at approximately 3 P.M. with a destination unknown to me, I was in the custody of two Luftwaffe MPs, on foot. We walked clear across town I think, across a little foot bridge with a frozen river underneath. There was a park with trees on each side of the river. There was some bomb damage here and there, but not total like I was to see later.

One of my two escorts soon left. He was the younger of the two and a gung-ho NAZI type. When departing, he patted his pistol and made me to understand that I would be shot if I didn't behave. So now I have but one MP with me. He was a big man, in his thirties I guessed. After the other one departed, this fellow started trying his very rusty English on me by pointing at some bombed out buildings, frowning, shaking his head and whatever it took to make his point. I got the message, and I replied that this looks just like London. He made me know that he was aware that the bombing of London was a drop in the bucket in comparison to what some cities in Germany were getting hit with. I replied with something about the V2s that were currently hitting London. He scoffed at that and went on to tell that his home town was Dusseldorf, and that only recently--he wrote in the snow--20,000 civilians had been killed in one raid. I didn't have an answer for that one. A few more blocks went by, and I asked if he was an officer. He laughed and said no, his rank was Sgt. Major. He had served on the Russian front as well as in France. He went on to say that his name was Henry Fischer. We were communicating pretty well by now, a little English and much sign language. He tells me that he took English in high school. He took out his wallet and showed me pictures of his family.

We must have walked for at least a half hour. Some ten year old boys with swastika armbands followed us for several minutes, heckling me. I did my best to ignore them, so they soon gave up. We finally reached our destination, which turned out to be a train depot. We went inside and to the ticket window. Words were spoken. The ticket agent gave me the usual dirty looks, handing the Sgt. some passes. Then we went to an outside bench to wait for the train. We were sitting for awhile when I got the urge for a BM. I made some comments about having to go, but the Sgt. obviously did not understand until I went through the motions of undoing my belt buckle. Ya Ya, he got the message and off we went to the stations men's room which was downstairs in the basement. I observed that it was a conventional men's room with urinals along one wall and stall-pay toilets along the other wall. The big difference between U.S. style and this was instead of coin-operated doors on the stalls, these were key-operated, and a lady with a change belt collected the fee, and then unlocked the stall. The Sgt approached the lady, pointed at me and told her my need. She gave me some awful dirty looks and said some dirty-sounding words, led us to an end stall which I'm sure was reserved for tramps and the likes. She unlocked the door, and sure enough, it was filthy, but I didn't complain. I had my BM while the Sgt. waited outside. Then we went back upstairs to the same bench, sat down and waited again.

Eventually the train came. We boarded and had an uneventful hour or so ride. We got off the train in another city. By now it is about dusk and the Sgt. walked us to a nearby cafe. He sat me in a chair against the wall while he stood at the bar and had a tall glass of beer. He had all of my belongings that had not ended up in the pockets of the 88 gunners. He was showing my wallet contents to the bartender, one of which was a snapshot of my best high school buddy who was now in the Navy and stationed at Pearl Harbor. The picture was of this friend, palm trees and hula girls. The Germans were getting a big laugh; they came to me and, pointing to the picture, asked "Havaii, Havaii??" I nodded my head yes. Then someone brought me a piece of toast with honey spread and a hot cup of coffee. I thanked them the best way I could and devoured the bread, and gulped the coffee. This was my first bite and drink since the 4 A.M. breakfast at Hethel.

"Jack Clark"

When we were finished with the coffee and snack and the Sgt. his beer, we went back on the streets. It was growing dark by now and there seemed to be lots of people on the streets, going where, I don't know. (Sunday evening Mass maybe). Everyone seemed to be well-dressed in Winter overcoats, etc. Everyone in uniform wore knee-high black boots—jack boots.

The Sgt. and I walked a short distance from the pub to the entrance of what turned out to be an underground bomb shelter. We went down a flight of stairs and entered a huge theater-like room with long rows of benches. There were a few families getting ready to spend the night. Everybody was bundled up as there was no heat. The Sgt. directed me to a bench across the room from other people. Then he went over to the group and joined in their conversation. From the stares in my direction, I must have been the main topic.

Maybe an hour later, the Sgt. came over to my side of the room and motioned me to follow. Back on the street, we resumed our walk to I didn't know where. I was glad to be outside again because I felt very much the villain in that bomb shelter along with all those apparently bombed out, homeless families.

Our next destination turned out to be the train station again. Apparently our train was about due, for we went out on the station platform and leaned against an iron railing. I was feeling quite comfortable with my situation, as the hot coffee and toast had worked wonders. My feet had returned to nearly normal color. I was looking around, taking in all the bomb damage, twirling the electric cord from my electric heated suit and apparently looking all too happy. A well-dressed middle-aged gent approached us and asked the Sgt if his prisoner was "Americana or English?" The Sgt answered, "Americana," and that lit the fuse. This person all but exploded, he threw a right fist at my face. I was quick enough to move my head to one side so that his fist only grazed my left ear. But in this few seconds, a crowd moved in--lynch mob-- and they had blood in their eyes--my blood. In seconds they surrounded us on three sides and left little doubt of their intentions.

The Sgt. came to my rescue. He whipped out his pistol and screamed at them. Whatever he said must have been very convincing because the crowd dispersed as fast as they'd gathered. The Sgt. returned his pistol to its holster and stared after the people. He was obviously a little shook up. I felt very much in his debt. After that I kept my eyes on the ground, for now I was fully aware of the burning hatred out there for me. I would possibly live longer if I could crawl back into the woodwork.

When the train arrived we crowded into a compartment. The Sgt. told me to sit down on the bench directly across from where he intended to sit. The only problem with this was a teenage girl and her mother occupied the two seats next to where I was directed to sit. And the train was crowded. There were no other choices. The mother of the girl raised a big fuss. She objected loudly to having a "Chicago gungster" next to her daughter. But again the Sgt. won the argument. I was directed again to sit down next to the girl, and he proceeded to sit down across from me. I made sure I didn't touch the girl. It was very dim light, and I couldn't see what she looked like anyway.

This train ride was about an hour long again, and it stopped at a tiny depot apparently out in the country. We got off at street level with the Sgt. leading the way. There was an old gent who got off also, and he was following behind me. He had his arms full, bags of groceries or whatever. He was having some difficulty maneuvering out of the depot but was close behind when we came to an iron gate. The Sgt. was first through. Then I was supposed to follow right behind, but instead I stopped to hold the spring-loaded gate open for the old gent with his arms full. The Sgt. turned around in time to see me assisting the old man, and I could tell he was pleased.

By now it must have been close to 11 P.M. We left this little station house and started down a road with about two feet of snow on the ground. We seemed to be out in the country as there were no lights anywhere, only the moon and the stars. The Sgt. seemed to know where he was going. I followed along, stepping in his tracks to avoid as much of the snow as possible with my open-toe sandals. We must have plodded along this way for at least a half hour when we came to some low buildings, one of which I could make out to be a hangar. I thought to myself this must be a Luftwaffe air station where I would be kept as a POW. We went inside and were met by another Luftwaffe person. The two of them talked briefly and then led me down a long hall lined with doorways, like an office hallway, only each door had a number on it. We stopped outside a door. The Corporal, or whatever he was, opened the door, stepped inside and pulled the chain turning on an overhead light. I was directed in. The room was about six by ten feet with a straw covered bunk on one side of the room. There were no windows. I entered, turned around and faced the two of them standing in the open doorway. Sgt. Major Henry Fischer offered me his hand, and I shook it. I felt like we were old friends--I owed my life to this man; I don't know what he felt toward me. It must have been a real drag for him to be ordered to leave home (?) this cold Sunday afternoon to escort a hated American around the Ruhr. In any case I felt good about the hand shake in front of a fellow Luftwaffe soldier.

This brought to an end "MY LONGEST DAY"--ever!! The two Germans took their leave, closing and locking the door behind them. I collapsed on the straw mattress. It must have been close to midnight by now, and I probably could have slept on concrete. I can still remember stretching out on that crude bunk. Each end was elevated, hospital-style. It was great, and I was very happy to be alive. I had come face to face with our MAKER at least a half dozen times in this one day and had been passed over each time. I went to sleep wondering what kind of duty the Germans might have in mind for me at this air station. I had no idea what POW life was all about; but I felt that having lived through this day, I could surely make it the rest of the way. My confidence was boundless.

The next morning a Luftwaffe guard came up the hall--I could hear the distinct clunk-clunk of his boots--stopped in front of my door, turned the key and swung it open. He didn't say a word, just delivered a piece of toast with honey and a cup of coffee. Then he left, locking the door behind him. Clunk-clunk back down the hall he went. From this activity I surmised that I was the only prisoner in this part of the building. I ate the toast, drank the coffee, which was lousy by the way, then sat down on the bunk and awaited the next event, whatever it may be. I couldn't guess how many hours went by when a German guard came clomp, clomp down the hall, stopped in front of my door and unlocked it. Motioning for me to follow, he clomped back up the hallway. Near the end of the hall we made a left turn to an outside exit, outside a short distance to an adjacent building and eventually into a huge gym-like room. There were no words spoken. The guard escorted me into this huge room, and then he turned around and left. I was wondering what I was supposed to be doing all by myself when another door opened and in came some other crew remnants that I did not recognize. A few more minutes went by and the door opened again. This time I was overjoyed, for into the room came Lt. Berthelsen, Lt. Riggles Sgt. Holdredge and Sgt.

Winter. Oh yes, the radar operator, Sgt. DeFalco was there also. All of these, except the tail gunner, were off the crowded flight deck, and I thought surely they had all died in the flaming wreck of Miss America. They were just as surprised to see me. The signs of happy reunion were unmistakable, and, of course, this was part of the German intelligence strategy.

Of the total number of prisoners taken on this raid, they wanted to know who belonged to what crew and aircraft. This was the simple way for them. They just put us all in one big room, then stood back and watched us sort ourselves out. Our pilot was wise to this game, and he tried to keep a straight face and direct me away with an arm wave, but it was too late. I was so happy to see them alive, I was all over them. By the time I wised up to what was going on, the Germans knew exactly what they wanted to know.

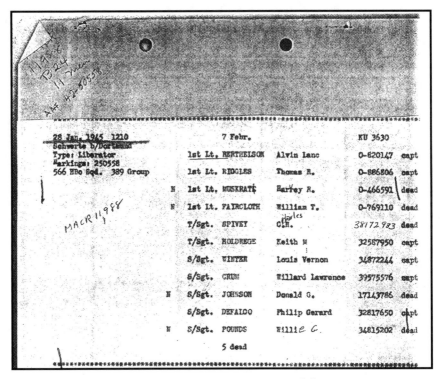

"German Document 7 Feb"

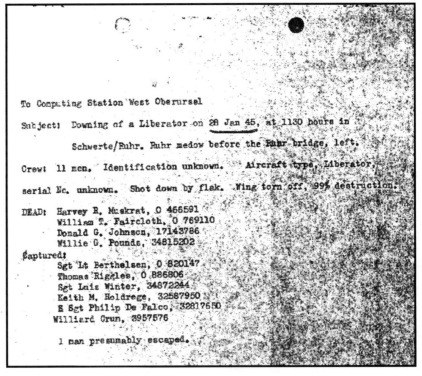

"Downing of Liberator"

Luftwaffe generated reports

Meldung über den Abschuß eines US-amerikanischen Flugzeuges			Abschuß-Nr. KU 3630		

Abschußtag und Zeit: 28.1.45 – 12.10

Abschußort: Schwerte b. Dortmund

Flugzeugtyp: Liberator

Meldende Dienststelle: Dortmund

B e s a t z u n g :

Name und Vornamen: Geburtstag und -ort:		Dienst-grad	Erk.-Marke:	gef.: verw.: tot:	Verbleib: welches Lager Art d. Verwundung Grablage
BERTHELSEN 1918	Alwin Lang USA	1.Lt.	O-820147	gef.	Dulag-Luft West
RIGGLEH 8.11.23	Thomas R. Wash. D.C.	1.Lt.	O-886806	gef.	Dulag-Luft West
DEFALCO 19.3.23	Philip Gerard Brooklyn, N.Y.	S/Sgt.	32617650	gef.	Dulag-Luft West
CHUM 26.2.25	Willard Lawrence USA	S/Sgt.	39575576	gef.	Dulag-Luft West
HOLDRIDGE 10.8.16	Keith M. N.Y. Mc Donough	T/Sgt.	32587950	gef.	Dulag-Luft West
WINTER 21.1.25	Louis Vernon Miss.	S/Sgt.	34872244	gef.	Dulag-Luft West

"German Report KU 3630"

Subsequent to this little session, I was again separated from the others, led down yet another long hallway to an office, and ushered in. A Luftwaffe officer who sat behind a desk, had the personal belongings of Sgt Spivey, our flight engineer, spread on the desk. He wanted me to identify them. The officer spoke very good English, and he asked me if I knew the man that these items belonged to. I was not told what happened to him, or even that he was dead, but there was not much room for doubt. He had written a letter to his wife the day before back at Hethel and had stuck it in his pocket and forgotten to mail it. The German had the letter on his desk. It was all crumpled up. It showed no signs of burning, or of blood, just very wrinkled and dirty. I supposed the expression on my face told all because I was asked no more questions. The letter had the return address of our bomb group, squadron, etc. So from this they knew our bomb group and squadron ID. Now he apparently had all of us accounted for.

IN REPLY REFER TO:
AG 201 Crum, Willard L.
   PC-N ETO 040

17 February 1945

Mrs. Maude Crum
14103 Gilmore Street
Van Nuys, California

Dear Mrs. Crum:

This letter is to confirm my recent telegram in which you were regretfully informed that your son, Staff Sergeant Willard L. Crum, 39,575,576, has been reported missing in action over Germany since 28 January 1945.

I know that added distress is caused by failure to receive more information or details. Therefore, I wish to assure you that at any time additional information is received it will be transmitted to you without delay, and, if in the meantime no additional information is received, I will again communicate with you at the expiration of three months. Also, it is the policy of the Commanding General of the Army Air Forces upon receipt of the "Missing Air Crew Report" to convey to you any details that might be contained in that report.

The term "missing in action" is used only to indicate that the whereabouts or status of an individual is not immediately known. It is not intended to convey the impression that the case is closed. I wish to emphasize that every effort is exerted continuously to clear up the status of our personnel. Under war conditions this is a difficult task as you must readily realize. Experience has shown that many persons reported missing in action are subsequently reported as prisoners of war, but as this information is furnished by countries with which we are at war, the War Department is helpless to expedite such reports.

The personal effects of an individual missing overseas are held by his unit for a period of time and are then sent to the Effects Quartermaster, Kansas City, Missouri, for disposition as designated by the soldier.

Permit me to extend to you my heartfelt sympathy during this period of uncertainty.

Sincerely yours,

J. A. ULIO
Major General
The Adjutant General

1 Inclosure
   Bulletin of Information

"War Dept MIA Letter"

This followed telegrams sent on Feb 1

When this unpleasant session was over, I was escorted back to my cell and was pleasantly surprised to find that I now had the company of Sgt's Winter and Holdredge. We were together for much of the duration of our captivity. But that is another whole story in itself.

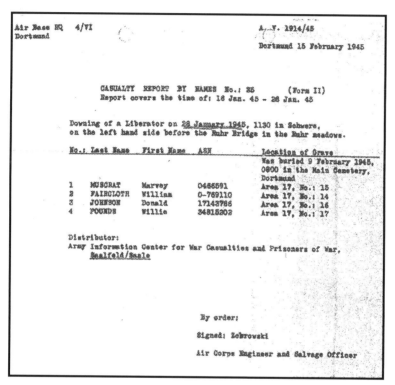

"*Dortmund Burial Report*"

I would only mention here that for the duration of the war, that is--February, March and April and the first week in May I was witness to incredible human misery. We American and British POWs had it bad, but it was a piece of cake relative to how the Russians and the Polish were treated. The Germans honored the Geneva Convention and the International Red Cross for POWs from member nations. But many of the eastern European countries had no part in either organization. Therefore, those POWs were treated little better than the Jews. That is, they were worked or starved to death and nobody cared which came first.

The destruction of most German cities was complete. We have all since seen photos of Nagasaki and Hiroshima and what the first atomic bombs did. Well, the cities of Germany didn't fare much better. The big difference was that in Germany it took over two years, and many hundreds of Allied aircraft and lives to accomplish the same destruction. Whole cities were wasted, maybe two or three cities each day, and night, around the clock, seven days a week and every day of the year including holidays, weather permitting. For the people in the cities, the bombing could be compared to a 7.0 earthquake over and over again. Terrifying!

The B29 fire bombing of Tokyo for several months preceding the August atomic bombing of Nagasaki and Hiroshima does not get much mention either. The fact is there were many thousands more casualties and the destruction was as complete. The point is atomic bombing does not deserve the reputation of being the only nasty weapon used in WW II. The atomic bomb's claim to fame was the speed at which it brought the war to an end and for this everyone on both sides--except for the Japanese war lords--was grateful.

Mankind should come to realize that wars, such as WW II, have to be a thing of the past. With the current missile technology, coupled with nuclear warheads, to allow any national differences to develop into full blown war, is suicidal for us all. Yet there are those little dictators around today who probably would not hesitate to begin something if they had the tools with which to do it. Can anyone speculate where we would all be today if Adolph had gotten his hands on an atomic warhead to load onto his V2??! TERRIBLE!! I also wince to think how we 8th AAF crews might have fared had Hitler put a little more emphasis on his electronic development and had those 88 shells fitted with a proximity fuse. I think that our stateside factories would have had a problem keeping up with replacement aircraft.

In conclusion, I wish to explain myself to my family and my many friends, to whom over the years, I literally clamed up when asked to talk about my war experience. The fact is, for many years I could not talk about it except to somebody who was there and had similar experiences. Now it is over fifty years later, and the whole experience seems like only yesterday. I feel that I owe it to anybody who might listen to tell about how utterly destructive war has become. These fifty+ years past, I have become friends and neighbors with German immigrants who were in Berlin, Stuttgart, Magdeburg, and many other German cities which were totally destroyed. They had to deal with the death and destruction, dodging our bombs, AND lynching the likes of myself when the opportunity presented itself. How does one sort these things out? Seems ridiculous, as in the case of Germans and Japanese, for four years we were killing each other, a couple of years later they are our Allies, friends and neighbors. The hatred generated by the bombing of cities, and the propaganda that accompanied same, was terrible. The German public was told by Hitler's propaganda minister, Goebbels, that all American bomber crews were one;, volunteers; two, Chicago gangsters; three, murderers of women and children; and four, terrorfliegers (terrorists). Therefore, civilians were free to execute or whatever, any American that came down from the skies. And further, any German officer, military or police, using a weapon on his own people to protect an American, would have to answer to him personally. And the people believed!

Lest we forget, PEOPLE ARE THE SAME THE WORLD OVER. It is the LEADERS of the world and their propaganda machines who must be ousted before they gain too much power over their people. The freedom of speech, especially in reference to the media, is all important. Once a government gets control of the media, beware! Propaganda may be the most important tool of war. I hate to think what the world would be today if Adolf Hitler would have had TV.

CHAPTER VII

KREIGIE

(Kreigie---German for POW)

One German soldier said to me, "For you, der var iss offer," (The war is over). Well, not quite. It is true that I was certainly through with flying combat missions. I had been expended. But now it was a matter of survival, and the Germans were in no position to provide for us other than to pen us up. On day three, we were trucked to a train station in Dortmund. There were about twenty of us, the remnants of three crews. We were loaded onto a civilian train, occupying three compartments with a Luftwaffe guard on each compartment. We traveled all night, arriving in the Frankfurt station early in the morning. There we were met by ten Luftwaffe guards armed with sub machine guns that marched us into the middle of the station rotunda and surrounded I think they were trying to impress the civilian population with their catch of "Chicago gungsters." We stood there for ten minutes or so before we were herded out an exit to a street car. The street car was crowded with people going to work. No matter, we were directed into the entrance to mingle with the civilians. Most of us had to stand in the aisle. One of the guards stood at each exit. We traveled east from the rail station for maybe a half an hour. When we reached our destination, we exited the street car and lined up in the street for a head count. We then marched a short distance to a fenced in area with a guard at the gate. The gate was opened and we filed in.

We were met by a German officer, who spoke very good English. He asked, "Who is the senior officer of this group?" A captain reluctantly spoke up saying, "I am a captain. I guess I am." The German shot back, "I am a major of the German Air Force and you will address me as Sir!" The poor captain answered, "Yes, Sir." It was all an attempt to scare hell out of us.

The German then asked if there were any among us who needed medical attention. We had one waist gunner in the group who was burned on the head pretty badly. He was wearing a bandage which was soaked through with puss. But he didn't want to leave the group to go to a hospital. He told of the fuel tanks on his plane, spewing gasoline and fire all over him. He said his chest chute was on fire. The last thing that he remembered was standing in the waist, trying to beat that fire out with his hands. Apparently the B24 exploded about that time for he woke up on the ground, very well singed but still alive. The rip cord on his chute was still in place. The fire had burned enough of the parachute encasement to allow the silk to exit and open. There were some holes burned in the silk which caused him to come down somewhat fast, so he sustained some internal injuries. The captain spoke for him, insisting that he get medical help. So he was separated from the rest of us. The remaining were split off and led away in small groups, then split off again. Co-pilot Riggles and I were paired off and led away. We were taken indoors and down a hallway to a cell and locked in. The inside of the cell was made like a small dungeon. This was to impress upon us what a horrible future we had. This holding cell turned out to be only temporary for the two of us were only there for an hour when they took Riggles away, leaving me to wonder if the firing squad was next, or what.

I didn't have long to wait. Soon a guard came for me and led me into another building, up a flight of stairs and down a long hallway that had many doorways. The guard stopped in front of one of them, opened it and directed me to enter. I walked in, the Kraut showed me a handle by the door, muttered something in German, and then he closed the door behind me and locked it.

It was a small cell with a straw covered bunk on one wall. There was a frosted glass window on the end opposite the door. There were no toilet facilities. That turned out to be what the handle was for, when you had to go, you pulled the handle, raising a flag in the hallway. Hopefully, Fritz would come, unlock the door and escort you down the hallway to the latrine. He always made sure there was no other prisoner using the facility because this was isolation where there was to be no communication with anyone.

Day one passed. In the morning Fritz came down the hall and pushed a bowl of barley soup through a small opening. He had a bucket and was serving each cell. No words were spoken. The soup was good nourishment, and it was hot which was good as there was no heat in the whole building. I put that soup down in a hurry as it was my first real food in several days. But I was content, for I was very happy to be alive. I was thinking of what a good job my ANGEL was doing. These Krauts were not scaring me.

Seven days of solitary confinement passed. Each day was the same. It was difficult to tell night from day except for the little sunlight which came through the window. I lay on that straw mattress, staring at the ceiling. I would jump up when it was feeding time. The menu was always the same—barley soup. On the eighth day, around mid-morning, a guard came to my door, opened it, and motioned me to follow him. We went down the hall, down the stairs, out the building, across the yard to another building. There I was led down a hall to an open door and motioned to enter. Then the guard stayed outside and closed the door.

A Luftwaffe officer sat behind a large desk. He told me to come in and sit down at the chair in front of the desk. The walls of the room were plastered with B17 and B24 drawings, complete with armament specifications. The officer spoke perfect English. He started right in. "Where are you from? California, I have been there. What wonderful oranges they grow there. When did you enter the AAF? Where did you take your basic training? Kearns, Utah. Oh yes, that's a terrible place." And he opens a book and reads off some statistics about Kearns. About the only directions I was ever given about being taken prisoner was give only your name, rank and serial number. But I didn't see any harm in telling him about my training days. He had the only important bit of information that I knew of-- my bomb group and squadron ID—which he got from the letter Spivey was carrying. So I talked. It was pleasant after seven days of no words with anybody. "Where did you go from Kearns? Lowery Field in Denver. And where did you take gunnery training? Harlingen Texas. And where did you become part of a flight crew? Westover Field. Then when did you leave for England? How many missions did you fly?" And that's when I shut up. I knew that information might be important to him. His next question was "Do you smoke?" When I said yes, he leaned over the desk and offered me a cigarette from a box. After I took one he lit it for me. I took a couple of puffs and nearly reeled to the floor it was so strong. He said they were American cigarettes. A minute or so went by, and he repeated "How many missions?" I shook my head NO and did not say anything. He said, "I already know, because I got the number from one of the others, but I need to confirm it." I said, "You tell me that number. I will tell you if it is correct." No way was he going to play that game. He slammed his fist on the table and hollered for the guard. When the guard came through the door, the officer said to me, "You will go back to that cell and rot unless you tell me what I want to know." He motioned to the guard to take me away. So back I went to the cell thinking I might be there for the duration.

The next morning I was taken out, given a shower and shave. Then I was photographed and fingerprinted. I was given a pair of U.S. flight boots, and that night taken to a train and shipped out along with about ten other prisoners. Winter was among the ten. Boarding the train, it was so black out I could not see my hand in front of my face. It was total BLACK-OUT, no lights allowed. The guard told us that if we promised no escape attempts, he would not take our boots. Everybody in the group agreed to his terms. We stumbled aboard single file and the train departed, for where we had no idea.

Next morning the train pulled into the small city of Wetzler. As our group exited the train, the guard took a head count then marched us out of the train depot and up the road to Dulag Luft. This was an established POW camp for Luftwaffe prisoners. With the double barbed wire fence and a guard tower on each corner, it looked formidable as we approached. The gate was opened, and we filed in. Once inside, there was another head count. Then the Germans put an American in charge of us to assign us a barracks and bunk. We also went through a line where a blanket was issued. I was issued a pair of GI high top shoes, GI overcoat, and one pair of socks, all provided by the American and Swiss Red Cross. Anybody in the group who had picked up lice was directed to the shower and head shave. We received a lecture about the rules and regulations set up by the Germans. Each man was given a "Kreiganspost" post card to send home to family (mine was received a year after I arrived home).

"Stalag Luft (air crew prison)" here

What a dismal place to be caged. It was early February, and it was cold. There were a few snowstorms. No matter what the weather, each morning we formed up outside for a head count. A German would parade in front of the five deep formations, waving his arms and counting as he walked. If his count came out correct, He then reported the number to the commandant. If it did not, then the count process was repeated. When they were satisfied that no one had escaped, the commandant would then read us the German slant of the news which was always a week old and very biased. The German retreat was never mentioned.

While standing for the head count, every other day we watched the changing of the guard. About fifty soldiers in a column of two across marched up the hill from the town below. They were always singing the same marching song as they progressed up the road to the front gate. When reaching the gate, they stopped singing. Years later, I found myself whistling this same tune while taking a morning shower.

The barracks were unheated except for one piece of coal per day for the pot bellied stove. We went to the mess hall twice daily for meals made from Red Cross parcels. Americans ran the kitchen, and they did a very good job of rationing out what was available. It was lean but no one went without. The main activity in the daytime was walking the perimeter which was a well marked path about ten feet inside of the barbed wire fence. There was a warning wire that ran about one foot parallel from the path. Prisoners were not to cross that warning wire. The guard in the tower was always watching and would start shooting. I spent much of my time in my overcoat, walking the perimeter.

The barracks were crowded and smoky. There were British air crews among us and I did not like their conversation. To hear them tell it, one would be led to believe that they alone were winning the war. At dusk we had to be inside with the window shutters closed and locked by Fritz. Big German Sheppard's were turned loose inside the compound to make sure that no prisoner would be wandering around outside his assigned barracks. It was a pretty miserable existence.

There was some excitement a couple of times. One day I was in a room having my hair cut. I was sitting on a stool facing a window which looked out to the perimeter walk and barbed wire fence. This was a nice sunny day, about noontime. A POW, right in front of my window, crossed the warning wire and climbed the ten foot high fence. He was on top of the inside fence when the guard in the tower fired the first shot. The POW dropped to the ground between the double fences, fought his way through the coils of barbed wire, and up the outside fence. When he was on top, the guard fired again. This time it was not a warning shot for it knocked the POW off the top of the fence, but he fell on the outside. He got up and ran towards the top of the hill and freedom. The guard fired a couple of more rifle shots but apparently missed. Then when the POW looked like he might get away and was about a hundred yards away, the guard put down his rifle and fired about twenty rounds from his machine gun. The POW dropped and went no further. The guard in the tower, an old timer, was waving his arms and hollering. He obviously did not like his job right now. At about the same time, half dozen guards with their dogs came around the corner in hot pursuit but they were not needed. The barber and

I watched the whole episode through that window and were dumbfounded. This was obviously a suicide.

It was no sooner over when Fritz came through hollering, "Efferybody OOUT" for headcount. The Germans were worried that this was some sort of diversion. We formed up, and Fritz went through the usual head count. The commandant stood in front to supervise. They kept us standing there to watch the guards carry in the body on a stretcher. I heard later that he was a newcomer who had not been sleeping, was talking and blaming himself for some of his crew being trapped and killed in a crippled B17.

On another day, the air raid sirens began wailing in the town down the hill. Fritz came through hollering the usual "EFFRERYBODY OOUT!" Outside we were herded into some trench type air raid shelters which were very crude, wet and muddy. We watched the whole show. A twelve plane squadron of B26's came over at about 10,000 feet and bombed the town. They had no fighter escort and after leaving the target, a Fock-Wolfe sneaked up behind them and knocked one of them down. Then the German came down and buzzed the POW camp. We watched three parachutes come out of the B26, so we expected that they would be brought to the camp. But that evening at roll call, we were informed by the guards that all three had been caught by civilians and hung.

Those were the only two days that stand out in my memory. The rest were very boring and dreary. Trying to stay warm, walking the perimeter, waiting for meal time were the main occupations. Then sometime in early March at night we could hear very distant artillery. U.S. troops were crossing the Rhine. The Germans began evacuation of the prison, 100 or so at a time, mostly at night. We would wake in the morning to find more barracks empty. I believe I was in nearly the last group to be shipped out.

For the trip each POW was given a Red Cross food parcel. My only possession other than the clothes on my back was my blanket. I rolled the food parcel in it and slung it on my shoulder. About fifty of us were formed up in a column late one afternoon, along with about six armed guards. The main gate was opened, and we marched down the hill to the town's railroad station. The whole group was squeezed into one car that had bars on the windows. Each compartment was designed for six passengers, but we managed to get in about twelve. We took turns stretching out in the overhead baggage rack. It was pretty uncomfortable, but it was good to be out of that boring prison.

HEADQUARTERS ARMY SERVICE FORCES
OFFICE OF THE PROVOST MARSHAL GENERAL
WASHINGTON 25, D. C.

AG

30 March 1945

RE: S/Sgt. Willard L. Crum
United States Prisoner of War
Interned by Germany
International Red Cross Directory
Geneva, Switzerland
Via: New York, New York

Mrs. Maude Crum
14103 Gilmore Street
Van Nuys, California

Dear Mrs. Crum:

The Provost Marshal General has directed me to supplement the information you received recently from the Adjutant General, concerning the above-named prisoner of war.

Information has been received which indicates that he is now interned as a prisoner of war by the German Government. The report received did not give his camp location. This conforms with the usual practice of the German Government not to report the address of a prisoner of war until he has been placed in a permanent camp. Past experience indicates that his camp address may not be reported to The American Prisoner of War Information Bureau until one to three months have elapsed from the time he was first reported a prisoner of war.

Pending receipt of his permanent address, you may direct letter mail to him by following instructions in the inclosed mailing circular and by addressing the envelope as illustrated thereon. A parcel label, and two tobacco labels, with instructions for their use, will be forwarded, without application on your part, when his permanent location is reported.

Sincerely yours,

Howard F. Bresee

HOWARD F. BRESEE
Colonel, CMP
Director, American Prisoner of War
Information Bureau

Incl
Mail Cir

"War Dept POW Letter"

PRISONERS OF WAR
Three Valley soldiers have been taken prisoners of war in Germany, the War Department announced this week. They are:
Staff Sgt. Willard L. Crum, 14103 Gilmore st., Van Nuys.
Pvt. Dale S. Kunkel, 1030 E. Orange Grove ave., Burbank.
Tech. 5 John A. Riddell, 6914 Day st., Tujunga.

"Newspaper POW notice"

Next morning we arrived at the city of Ulm. Our car was disconnected from the train and left sitting in the demolished railroad terminal. I think the Germans were hoping the terminal would be bombed, then they would not have to bother with us anymore. We sweated that whole day out. The whole terminal was a mess of broken concrete, twisted rails and dead locomotives.

Through the barred window, a couple of us were watching a small group of Russian women prisoners with picks working nearby. A Gestapo guard watched over them. The women were dressed in blankets tied around them, including their feet. One of the women, seeing our POW car, put down her pick and held up her fingers in the V for victory sign. The Gestapo told her to get back to work, I presume, but the woman instead bad mouthed him. The only word I could understand was "Hitler." The guard bent over, picked up a loose brick and threw it at her. She side stepped, so the brick missed. She then picked up her pick and resumed picking at a piece of concrete.

A very short time later, the city air raid sirens started wailing. The work group disappeared, with the guard being first. Fortunately for us POW's in that rail car, the sirens turned out to be a false alarm for soon the "all clear" sounded. My Angel was still with me.

Sometime in the night, our car was attached to a train, and we continued in a southerly direction. The next day, the train arrived in the city of Nuremburg. The entrance to our rail car was unlocked by some Luftwaffe guards and the group exited, formed up for the usual head count, then marched off through the bombed out city. There were not many buildings left standing, and those that were appeared to be empty hulks. We walked past one remnant of a block long building. Out in the middle, all by it self sat a whole Pratt-Whitney, like it had just dropped from the sky. There were no signs of the rest of the plane from which it came.

This turned out to be a three mile walk to where ever they were taking us. We walked past the famous Nuremberg stadium and on out into the countryside. We finally arrived at the prison camp. We were standing in the roadway in front of the commandant's office when along came a work detail of a dozen ragged looking Russian prisoners, accompanied by a couple of guards. As soon as the Russians spotted the cigarette butts scattered at our feet, they broke ranks and literally dived for every butt they could find. All the time the German guards were screaming at them to get back into ranks. There was much commotion for a few seconds, then it was over and the work detail continued on past us and on down the little road.

Soon we were marched on along the fence toward the main gate. There were several POW's hanging on the inside of the fence waiting to greet us newcomers. Among those I spotted was Lt. Berthelsen. He did not look happy. He had already been here for two weeks. He said to me, "This place is terrible." When I asked what was wrong, he answered, "There is nothing to eat." Our group moved on down to the gate where we were ushered into a big empty barn like building which was to be home for the next month.

Berthelsen was not kidding; this place was terrible. Even the security was bad with only a single broken down wire fence--no warning wire and no guard towers at the corners. It was apparently some sort of "has been concentration camp" for it was filthy and loaded with lice. Some of the buildings had fleas. There was no Red Cross establishment so when my travel parcel ran out, it was mighty slim pickings. A horse drawn farm wagon came through the gate each morning, with bread loaves piled high in the bed. The loaves were taken someplace and sliced up, then distributed by guards to each barracks. Each man received one slice. That was the day's nourishment which might have been adequate except the bread was fifty percent sawdust. Maybe twice a week we were treated to watered-down potato peel soup, doled out from a five gallon bucket by a German. Each man had a tin can saved from a food parcel for the soup. But there were no spoons, so the soup had to be drunk from the can. My ingenuity came in handy at this time for I scrounged a tin can lid which I shaped concave--sort of like a spoon. Then I found a piece of rusty wire which I fastened to the spoon and used it for the handle. Very crude but it worked. I used it for the duration of my POW days.

Life was miserable here. The building that I shared with about a hundred others was four walls and a roof. There was a pot-bellied stove in one corner near the door. Each man used his blanket to stake out a piece of the floor to call his bed. At night, as I lay wrapped in my blanket, the lice started their games. They were called lice, but they were more like tiny white crabs that nested in the hairy places on the body. When the body was quiet like in trying to sleep, these guys started their travel, from one hairy location to another, like from the crotch to the armpits and back again. This made going to sleep very difficult. In the daytime, when the sun came out, I spent most of my time outside, stripped off, picking the little varmints and their eggs, out of my clothes. It did not help too much, but it was something to do. One day I carried my blanket out to shake and air it; but it was so rotten that when I tried to shake it, it started coming apart. I had to give that up. That blanket had a lot of miles on it before I got it.

The second week of this I noticed that standing was becoming a chore. It was better to sit or sleep to conserve energy. The guard came around in the morning, unlocked the door and delivered our ration of bread. He also brought two pieces of coal for the stove. This was reveille. It was out of the blanket and line up for that piece of lousy sawdust bread. Next was to crowd around the pot bellied stove which had about ten feet of horizontal smoke stack before turning right angle toward the ceiling. Many of us made a practice of laying our slice of bread on that horizontal stack to warm it. This let the imagination work to make you think you were really getting something to eat, and it took some discipline to watch your ration lay there heating and not grab it off and gobble it down.

Black Bread Recipe

Former prisoners of war of Nazi Germany may be interested in this recipe for World War II Black Bread. This recipe comes from the official record from the Food Providing Ministry published, as Top Secret Berlin 24.XI-1941 from the Director of Ministry Herr Mansfeld and Herr Moritz. It was agreed that the best mixture to bake black bread was:

- 50% bruised rye grain
- 20% sliced sugar beets
- 20% tree flour (saw dust)
- 10% minced leaves and straw

From our own experiences with black bread, we also saw bits of glass and sand. Someone was cheating on the recipe!

"Black Bread"

After the breakfast (?), it was outside to sit in the sun if the sun was out. I did not do much walking of the perimeter, but one day I was out along the north fence. A German officer, accompanied by a Japanese officer, in full dress uniform complete with sword, were strolling along the outside of the fence. The Japanese looked all too happy observing us starving Americans, and I thought of spitting in his face. We were that close, him on the outside and me on the inside. That three foot sword at his side deterred me.

Another memorable event happened one day when Fritz came around with a five gallon bucket of soup. Everybody ran for their soup can, and then fell in line to get his can filled. This time it was not the usual potato peel stuff. It looked like boiled hominy kernels, or yellow peas. But each pea had a white tail which resembled a sprout. The German doled out each man's ration outdoors, and then most of us went inside to consume the soup. I no sooner just got started on mine when somebody examined his can full and came out spitting. He shouted, "Hey, those peas have worms." Then everybody started taking a close look at those peas with the white tail. Instead of looking closer, I walked to a dark corner of the room and enjoyed my soup. It was hot and too watery to worry about a few bugs. In fact, I was given a couple of others' rations. I stayed in my dark corner and consumed them also.

Three weeks of this went by. I was getting pretty weak. I noticed my hair falling out. My teeth had several cavities near the gums. It was becoming obvious that this was a starvation diet, and something better happen soon. It did. One day a Swiss Red Cross representative came through the camp. He inspected the barracks and conditions in general. About two days later, a big GMC, all white with big RED CROSSES painted all over it, came to the gate and unloaded food parcels. The ornery Germans took their time passing them out. They opened each package, punching an inspection hole in each of the cans.

It was late in the afternoon when each POW received one package. What a party we had. A big swap meet took place almost immediately. No one wanted the one pound can of powdered milk. Those who didn't smoke were trading off cigarettes for candy bars. The one pound box of Santa Clara Valley Prunes was going pretty cheap. I never was a wheeler and dealer, so I went with what the Red Cross dealt me.

There were two candy bars in each parcel. I think everybody consumed one or both that evening. That was a mistake for shortly after lights out and the battle of the lice had begun, those chocolate bars struck. And there was no indoor plumbing. In fact there was no plumbing anyplace in the camp--only slit trenches with a roof overhead. At lights out plus five, the first man with an urgent call made it to the door and hollered at the guard to open up. The guard opened the door and let him out, then closed it. I could hear him securing the latch. He no sooner completed the task when the second and then the third man had to go, banging on the door to get out. The guard was very busy for awhile. He finally gave up locking the door. The parade to the outdoors lasted most of the night. In the morning, the grounds around the barracks were one big mess. No one tried to make it to the latrine. Those chocolate bars were the beginning of my problem with dysentery. I was never constipated again for the duration and until long after I was home.

The Red Cross agent also arranged for showers. They apparently hauled in coal to heat enough water to provide each man in the camp with a three minute shower. Everybody was busy washing out their one pair of socks and underwear in preparation. The camp was divided into groups of approximately fifty men. When our turn came, the main gate was opened, and we marched out. The shower was a few hundred yards east of the camp and past a women's prison. They hung on the fence and waved at us as we passed. I think they were mostly Russians. We came to the showers which consisted of a big open sided tent with fifty overhead shower heads. We were told, three minutes of hot water. At the end of three minutes, the hot goes off. Everybody stripped off and found an empty shower head. When everyone was in place, the water was turned on. It was glorious while it lasted. I don't remember having a towel but this was the end of March and the days were warming. So we probably air dried before putting our dirty clothes back on. We marched back to the prison, the gates were opened, and we filed in. Another group was waiting for their turn at the shower.

Another few days went by when the gates were swung open to let in a group of about fifty Serb prisoners. They were a sight. They wore white robe uniforms, with a red hat complete with tassel. They wasted no time in setting up living accommodations which consisted of a huge circus type of tent. They each set up their bed roll in neat rows around the inside perimeter of the tent. That being accomplished, they let it be known they were ready to swap whatever. I went looking for a toothbrush, and I found one. This toothless Serb sat on his blanket with a few items spread out before him. Among the items was a toothbrush. I jumped the gun and held up two packs of Camels

"Behind the Wire"

The Serb all but came unglued taking possession of those Camels and handing me the toothbrush. I probably could have had the toothbrush for two cigarettes instead of two packs. There was no conversation, only sign language. I watched him open one pack, took out one cigarette, pulled out a pocket knife, and cut it into four pieces. He put one piece into a cigarette holder and lit up. He smoked that thing down to ashes. Anyway, I got a toothbrush, maybe slightly used but certainly better than none. I went back to my barracks, retrieved a piece of soap from my food parcel and went back outside to the water faucet to have a good tooth brushing session. It was then that I found an upper tooth was rotting off right at the gum line. I had to ignore it.

In the last week of March, one night about 11 P.M., the air raid sirens started wailing. Soon after that some nearby 88mm anti aircraft guns started thundering. And shortly thereafter, we could hear the British Lancaster's overhead. They were giving Nuremberg a working over. Since our camp was only three miles west of the city, we were concerned that we could catch a stray bomb. The British always bombed at night. They used a pathfinder method in which a lead bomber would find and mark out the target with flares. Then the rest of the bombers would follow single file, and one by one, dropping their bombs into the marked area. The air raid lasted for over an hour, and then all grew quiet as the last of the bomber stream left. Afterward the same wailing siren sounds with a short blast to announce the "all Clear."

Subsequent to the Nuremberg bombing, around the last days of March, the Germans began evacuating the camp in groups of approximately 200 POW's. Apparently, they were determined that our advancing ground forces would not liberate us. Approximately a week later our barracks was among the last to move out. Each man was issued a Red Cross parcel. We rolled our blanket, slinging it over the shoulder. Eating equipment (tin cans) was hung from the belt. The Germans informed us that this would be a long hike with no train rides. I was happy to be out of this place and on the road. It felt like a bit of freedom. I was feeling stronger after a few days of decent nourishment from the food parcels. So we formed up in columns of four, the gates were swung open. Out we went, headed south down a little country road. The little road led us up a long hill. At the crest of the hill, there was a small church. This is where we spent the first night. I remember entering the front door, then scrambling for the altar with the nice soft carpet. I slept on a wooden pew. I don't think any of us had any problem sleeping that first night out. The six hours of walking, mostly uphill, was exhausting.

Next morning, we formed up again and continued on down that little country road. The countryside was beautiful, with spring definitely upon us. The Germans did not bother with a head count anymore. They did not have to for everyone knew we were just ahead of the combat zone and no one wanted to get mixed into that to maybe get shot by a retreating German or worse yet, an advancing American. The only semblance to safety was to stay with the large numbers. In fact, the German guards accompanying us were staying pretty close to us POW's. As the march went on, they became friendlier. Hitler had put out the word that there was to be no surrendering. He had SS troupes bringing up the rear who were supposed to shoot any German soldier that did not stand and fight. So here was this small number of middle-aged Luftwaffe guards assigned to keep us out ahead of the big retreat. We were their excuse for retreating. What chaos.

On the second day out, I would guess we were no more than twenty miles south of Nuremberg. In the early afternoon, several squadrons of B24's flew directly overhead. They were bombing Nuremberg and apparently using 1000 pound bombs. We were out of hearing range of the bombs but looking up at the bits of blue sky; I saw the shock waves from a bomb blast. Very strange.

Fortunately for us it was spring. We did spend a couple of days walking in the rain. I remember one day walking until after dark in the rain and unable to reach any shelter. The guards called a halt, so we all scattered to find any shelter around. It was pitch black. The best I could find was a wood pile of scrap lumber. I was tired, lay down, pulled a BOARD over me and went to sleep. The next morning the rain had turned to a slow drizzle. The Germans rounded us up on the road, and we continued on. I don't know why all of us did not get pneumonia. Usually the day's march was planned so that we reached a town at or before dark. Fritz would go ahead and tell the priest of the local church that his building was to provide shelter for a couple hundred POWs that night. We would follow into town, parade into the church, and flop. One stop of this type was in a small city. The Catholic Church was old and very extravagant with lots of gold figures and thick red carpeting on the altar. Our group arrived there shortly after dark with no chance to get familiar with the surroundings, such as where's the latrine. Since most of us had dysentery, this was pretty important.

As usual, I was too slow to stake out a place on the altar, so I pitched my blanket in the aisle on a tile floor. No matter, I was tired and sleep came fast. But this had been one of those days of walking in the rain, and I was awakened by many men coughing. Once awake, my case of dysentery was calling. I sat up and looked around. It was so dark; the only thing visible was the guard standing at the door smoking a cigarette. I stood up and stumbled over toward that cigarette, asking, "Where is the shyzen housen?" (This was the only German language that I learned.) The guard pointed out the general direction, and that's all I could get out of him. This was a blacked out city, and it was BLACK outdoors. I walked fifty feet in the dark and could find no outhouse. By now the need was urgent, so I dropped my drawers and had my BM. I somehow found my way back to the front door and to my blanket and slept through the rest of the night. In the morning, I went back out the front door and was surprised to see a beautiful little churchyard with white picket fence separating churchyard from the street. There were civilians on the street side of the little white fence. They were not happy. Obviously, there had been many others that had the same problem as me during the night and that neat little churchyard was littered with little piles of turds. In fact, there were a couple of POWs squatted down adding to the mess.

For some unknown reason, the guards held us at this churchyard all morning. So along about midmorning when I needed my next BM, I dropped my drawers again and went at it. I was half way through when a German officer and his little girl came down the path. The officer frowned and said in perfect English, "You should be ashamed of yourself." Two POWs sitting near me eating from their food parcel spoke up saying, "He can't help it." I thought for a minute I was going to get a big black boot in the face. I felt embarrassed for the little girl.

About the second week on the road, we ran out of the Black Forest area and into open farmland. It was better as there were these ancient little villages, each with a tiny church in the center, surrounded by farm houses and barns. Our guards would tell the farmer to move over and open up his barn and barnyard to us. So we got to sleep in the hay with a good roof overhead. In the morning, there were wood scraps to be gathered for a campfire to warm food from the food parcels. Also, we traded soap and cigarettes for eggs which we cooked in our tin cans. One such stopover, a buddy and I prowled through this farmer's barn and found a barrel of sauerkraut. We helped ourselves to some. Also we found the farmer's cow tied up in her stall. My buddy milked her into a dirty can. Unfortunately, it was late in the day so the cow had already been milked, but we got half a can which we shared. It tasted like a bit of heaven.

Our group was spread out along this open road one day when some one sounded the alarm. I looked behind me in time to see a P51 coming down the road. I hit the dirt along with all the rest, including the guards. Fortunately the P51 did not fire a shot. The next day, the same P51 came, but this time he flew across the road instead of coming up behind us. He waved at us as he crossed over. He was only about twenty-five feet off the ground.

On another day on down the road we were entering a small town. It was a bright sunny day with fluffy white clouds overhead. There were fighters circling above the clouds and now and then I got a glimpse of P47s through a break in the clouds. An ancient flatbed farm truck passed our group, chugging down the little road. The truck was just out of sight when someone sounded the alarm "HIT THE DIRT." I looked back over my shoulder just in time to see the leader of a five plane squadron of P47s, in a 45 degree dive. The pilot had just released a 500 pound bomb. The bomb had cleared the P47, and was arcing down toward a military train, hidden in trees on a siding track about 500 yards to the west of us. I had not noticed it until the attack, but now it came to life in an attempt to defend itself. It had a flat car with a four gun battery of 20 mm cannons which opened up on the P47s. All of a sudden, the countryside was very noisy. But this was too close to enjoy observing the Germans taking a licking; all of us dived for cover. Alongside the road there was drainage ditch which filled with bodies very fast. I was late, so I walked across the bodies, and then dived behind a rock wall that paralleled the far side of the ditch. It was all over in less than a minute. When it grew quiet, we came back to the road and lined up again to resume the walk. The guys that had made it to the ditch first ended up on the bottom, under four or five others. They were a mess, but lucky that they did not drown as the ditch had water in the bottom.

A short distance down the road, we came upon the flatbed truck. The driver was still hiding and nowhere in sight He had bailed out of the open air vehicle and left it chugging down the road thinking those P47s was after him. The driver-less truck had plowed into a tree and stopped, but the radiator was mashed in, still blowing steam as we passed. This was another victim of the attack.

Yet another nice sunny warm day on the road, I think it was early afternoon, one of the guards was happy to inform us that our President was dead. No details, only that Roosevelt was dead. This was a blow to our moral which wasn't the greatest anyway.

Hitler Wanted to Kill All PWs

The Swiss Radio confirmed yesterday reports that in the last days of the war Adolf Hitler ordered all Allied prisoners of war shot.

Heard by BBC in London, the radio quoted Dr. Burckhardt, president of the International Red Cross. He said that the Wehrmacht had refused to carry out the order and that in March he met representatives of Heinrich Himmler _____ for the Red Cross to _____ PW _____ and prevent any last minute executions.

Last March, at the time of Dr. Burckhardt's visit to Germany, reports that Allied prisoners in Germany would be killed were widespread, but Himmler was blamed at that time. The reports never were officially recognized because of Allied concern over what might happen if Burckhardt's mission were a failure.

Dr. Burckhardt also said that Hitler always had wanted to renounce the International Conventions relating to prisoners of war, and that toward the last days of his life, his temper steadily grew worse.

"Hitler Edict"

130

The third week on the road, there was evidence that the U.S. ground forces were not too far behind us. One day, we crossed a bridge where German troops had cut a hole in the concrete pavement and were preparing a 500 pound bomb to lower into the hole to blow the bridge. The bomb looked like one of ours. Maybe it was one that the crew armorer had missed pulling the safety pin. Or maybe a bomber was shot down before reaching the target. In any case, I sure was curious as to how they got that bomb.

On down the road a little way, German troops were building a road block. They had logs laid across the road, and they were in the process of stacking them one on top of the other. We were detoured around without any problem and continued on down the road. It was a good sign. I wished our troops would hurry up and catch us. Our group was obviously bringing up the rear. It sure would be nice if somehow we cold be overtaken.

One day about dark, we were still walking. Louis Winter and I were side by side in the column when he grabbed my arm, crying out in pain. The two of us dropped to the roadside. Winter said he could not go on. He had very bad stomach cramps. I told him that I would stay with him. We were debating what to do and where to hide when along came the guards. The four of them spotted us and stopped. They were debating what to do with us when Winter spoke up and said that he was ok now and could go on. We both stood up got back on the road and continued on with the four Germans right behind.

Finally, at the end of three weeks on the road, we reached our destination. It turned out to be a huge POW camp near the village of Mooseburg, about sixteen miles north of Munich. It was labeled Stalag V11A. It was crowded. There were prisoners of all the Allied nations. There were thousands of each nationality including Russians, all gathered in this huge fenced in area. There were no barracks left when my group arrived so we were put in a huge tent that leaked when it rained. In fact it flooded in the middle of the night when it rained hard. I woke up to find an inch of water surrounding my one inch of straw mattress. Next day, we dug a drainage ditch around the outside. But there was no more rain.

On April 28th, the word came that Hitler had committed suicide. Good for him. He should have done it months ago as at this date, the whole German nation was in ruins. Let everybody be sure, there was no one unhappy about that piece of news. What a calamity. This one man, almost single handedly, had committed suicide not only for himself, but for the whole German Nation. The cities were flattened, the bridges were down, the churches and hospitals were in ruins. What was left of their military was on the run and surrendering at every opportunity. They could have laid down their arms and quit months ago, saving much of the destruction, but for the iron rule of the one nut. I often think what a difference in my life, and thousands of others, too, had the assassination attempt way back in July, been successful. The fickle finger of fate again. The fighting at that time was in France as it was shortly after D Day. The Russian front was still in Poland. Probably a million or more people would have survived the war had Adolph died on that day back in July

CHAPTER VIII

LIBERATION

The dysentery was taking its toll on me. My stomach was no longer able to digest anything except the powdered milk and the prunes. I was becoming dehydrated as the more water I drank, the worse the dysentery. I belched one day and Winter who was standing nearby, said it smelled like the worst fart he had ever smelled.

It is a good thing for me that it was about all over. I was there one week when on Sunday, April 29th, we heard some small arms fire and a couple of artillery shells exploding. We laid low until the firing stopped. Then it was over. Patton's armored vehicles drove down the outside of the fence. There were GIs riding the vehicles. Most of us were crying, big tears, along with cheering the arrival of our saviors. The Nazi flag came down and the Stars and Stripes went up. I don't know when I have ever been happier.

The arrival of Patton's 14th Armored Division was about noon on April 29th. It was an exciting day. The Russian POWs grouped together at the east end of the camp, tore down the fence, stormed down the hill to the village below. I heard that they razed the town. The French group followed the Russians down the hill. They came back a few hours later with a goat slung from a pole and carried by two men. They built a big fire and barbecued the goat. They must also have found some wine for the party went on into the night. I felt too weak to venture out, so I watched the celebrating from within the camp. I did not want to take a chance on getting into any kind of danger at this late time. I did go exploring into the German headquarters building which was now deserted. There were several of us in there, going through the file cabinets. The files were generated by the Luftwaffe, apparently at the interrogation center at Frankfort. I did not have any trouble finding my own record for they were all in neat alphabetical order. There was the mug shot, German issued serial number, several entries of where I was captured, aircraft and type and last but not least, the comment "gut soldier". Apparently, I earned that for not telling the interrogator all he wanted to know. I helped myself to that record and carried it with me all the way to Marysville California, and then I stupidly left it on the train where I was dropped off after the trip across country on the way home.

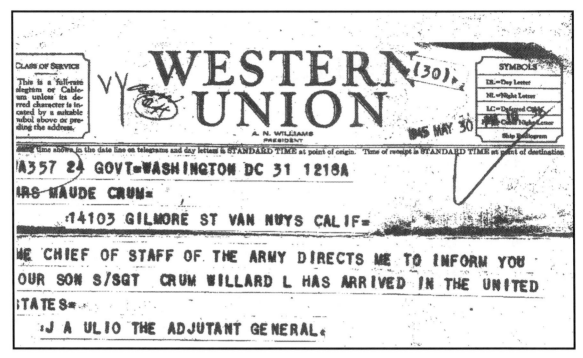

"Telegram"

The next day was bright and sunny. Most everybody in my tent left the camp and went hunting, mostly for food but that led to other things. They came back with all kinds of loot, taken from German homes. One character came back with an ancient armored suit, complete with helmet. I went outside the camp where I located a field kitchen set up for the ground troops. I talked to the mess sergeant who explained that he could not provide for the POWs. I told him that I understood, but I sure was hungry. He went inside the tent kitchen and came back with a three pound chunk of cheese and handed it to me. I chewed on that chunk of cheese for two days and guess what, my dysentery left me and my stomach began behaving again. That big piece of cheese was great medicine for malnutrition and dysentery.

Next day I wandered outside of the camp and found an Army Field Hospital. My buddy and I got in the chow line at breakfast where they were serving hot oatmeal with powdered milk. I had a bowl full which tasted like a bit of heaven. No one objected even though the two of us were easily distinguished as POWs in our filth. The oatmeal worked wonders for me. Along with the cheese, I began to get my strength back. I was back in that hospital chow line the next morning. Then my friend and I decided to do some sightseeing. We hitched a ride with an artillery truck, crossed the Danube and continued on to Landshut, a fair sized city. Our ground troops were bivouacked here and had things well under control, so we felt safe. We found a group of GIs occupying an upstairs German apartment. They invited us in for a bath. Upon reaching the top of the stairs, there were three or four GIs playing with some German kid's toy steam engine.

My friend and I took turns at the bath tub. One of the soldiers gave me some clean underwear and socks for which I was eternally grateful. I wish I had written down his name. It felt so good to feel clean again. They also gave us some "C" rations. Then we started back for the camp to be sure to be back before nightfall. It was a real pleasure, having all of this freedom, especially with the diminished dysentery.

On May the 6th, Berthelsen came to the tent with word that we were to be evacuated the next day. Alleluia!! It did not take much getting ready for all of my worldly belongings consisted of a rotting blanket, tin can, tooth brush and now my German POW service record. Next morning, I was out there early and in line to climb aboard the truck which was to take us to an airfield at Regansburg. I don't remember much about that part of the journey except that I got separated from the others of my crew, and I was with the same buddy that I had been hanging out with for the past few days. No matter, I was getting out of here and that's all that mattered.

My truck load arrived at the dirt airstrip at Regansburg in the afternoon. There were about twenty C47s shuttling POWs out of Germany to Camp Lucky Strike in France. We were lined up in groups to await our turn for an empty C47 returning from France for another group. My group did not make it before it started getting dark. These airstrips were not equipped for night flying, so we were told to hang out the best we could for the night and be back here to the airstrip in the morning. I chose to hang out with a group of six, one of which spoke pretty good German. The six of us found a nearby farmhouse and knocked on the heavy wooden door to ask if we could sleep in the barn. Instead, the farmer asked us in. It was a memorable experience. Only a few days ago, he and his family were our enemies. Now that Hitler was out of the way, we could be friends with no hard feelings. There were three of them, the farmer, his wife and a beautiful daughter in her mid twenties. She, through our interpreter, told us that she was married to a German soldier that was in the thick of the Battle of the Bulge, and she had not heard from him now for a couple of months.

We talked, via interpreter, until about 9:00 P.M. It was a little awkward but very hospitable. This was one of those ancient farmhouses with thick mud walls, candle light; and no indoor plumbing. The water supply was a hand pump and well. The wife showed us to a spare bedroom, lit a candle lantern for us, and then departed. There was only one bed so we drew straws to see who got the bed. I won. I crawled into that bed that had a goose feather mattress and blanket. It felt like a bit of HEAVEN. The other guys found a place on the floor. Next morning, we were up and out early so we would not miss that first flight out. We said goodbye to the farmer and his family, thanked him for his hospitality and headed back to the airstrip, arriving there in time to get onto the first C47 out.

As I recall, it was about an hour flight to an airfield in France. Shortly after landing there we were loaded into trucks for the trip to Camp Lucky Strike. This part of the journey took us through several small French villages where people were out waving at us as the truck passed through. Someone finally told us that the Germans had signed the surrender. The war in Europe was OVER. May the 8th, 1945, was a day that will live forever in my heart. **VE DAY** **(victory in Europe)**

Our truck arrived at Camp Lucky Strike in the afternoon. Everything was highly organized, ready and waiting for us. The first stop was de-lousing. We were herded down a fenced corridor, stripping off clothing as we walked. Clothing was tossed over the fence into a pile. At the end of the corridor were the showers with plenty of good strong GI soap to annihilate the lice and their eggs. There was no time limit on the hot water. It was a bit of heaven. After completing the shower, it was on out the exit to the new clothing issue--new sun-tan uniform, top to bottom, including new shoes. It felt great to get clean again.

Next stop was the chow line for by this time it was late afternoon. The mess hall was run by German POWs. What a switch. Now we could give THEM a hard time. But I don't think anybody did. They dished out the fried chicken until you told them to stop. I had my tray piled high, sat down at a table and went for it. This was my first real meal in over three months. I tried to make up for lost time. I helped a couple of others at the table, who couldn't finish theirs.

We were assigned a tent and bunk to sleep on. It was a six man Army tent, and a GI canvas cot. This was great also. I slept like a rock. Next day, one of our activities was to fill out a post card to home, to inform the home front of the safe arrival from Germany. Then there was the interrogation process. The survivors of our crew were gathered at a table where an interrogation officer interviewed us as to our treatment and any light we could shed on the five crew members who were still listed as MIA. I was the only one that had any positive information about Muskrat and Faircloth, in that I knew that they escaped from the spinning B24 just ahead of myself. I had seen two open parachutes above my own, and I was reasonably sure that it was them. Then there was the identification of Spivey's dog tags and pocket items that I was called upon to do by the German Luftwaffe officer.

Years later, an acquaintance investigating the MIAs of that day (there were seven B24s lost on that target--times ten men each. About twenty of us showed up as

POWs, which left approximately fifty MIA). He found that our B24 crashed into the edge of an open field near the village of Schwerte, about twenty miles south of Dortmund. The bodies of Muskrat and Faircloth were found near the crash site, indicating the two open parachutes that I had seen were empty so the two of them fell with no chute. The two of them had a bad habit of taking off on a mission with their leg straps undone, as a matter of comfort. VERY BAD HABIT. Pilot Berthelsen also jumped with leg straps undone, but by some miracle he managed to stay with the chute when it opened. Apparently the two waist gunners, Pounds and Johnson, perished in the flaming wreckage. Spivey remains on the MIA list. Why the Luftwaffe never informed our government of his death I do not know. I suspect they were covering for a lynching by civilians. The US military investigation performed after hostilities ceased, list two bodies decapitated and buried under a bridge, and identified them as Muskrat and Faircloth. But the Germans were not too careful about identifying the dead. They made a practice of confiscating dog tags immediately upon capture which could result in some confusion in the case of the dead. As for Spivey, there is also the story that he may have been injured and taken to a hospital.

Chapter IX

HOMEWARD BOUND

The stay at Camp Lucky Strike lasted about a week while we were awaiting a ship for the US. I was separated from the rest of my crew as the ship manifest was organized by destination, East Coast, West Coast, Mid West, etc. So I had to make new friends again. Who cares, I'm on my way HOME. This was the last time I was ever to see Sgt's Winter and Holdredge.

I boarded a ship which was to dock in Boston in about ten days I was told. The ship sailed from Le Havre, France. I noted that this city was pretty well flattened, just as were the cities of Germany. Also, once aboard ship, I saw the harbor was littered with half sunken ships. Such destruction.

The ship made a short stop at South Hampton, England, to pick up hospitalized GIs. When they were finished loading, the ship steamed out of the harbor and out into the Atlantic. The weather was good, so I spent much of my time out on deck as things were pretty crowded below. At night there was no smoking allowed on deck as there were still some German subs loose that had not surrendered.

The thing that I remember best about the boat trip was stuffing myself at every meal. Since this was a hospital ship, the food was excellent, and I made the most of it. In fact, I volunteered to work in the kitchen so that I could get extra pie and ice cream. That lasted to somewhere into the middle of the Atlantic. Then one night at the evening meal as I was working my way through a plateful, I looked up and noted that the dining room lights were dimmed. The next thing I knew, I was laying on the floor looking up to several faces. I had totally passed out. Some fellow passengers were bent over me, getting ready to carry me out. I got up by myself, explaining that I slipped and fell, knocking myself out on the steel deck. But I knew what really happened. I was on my way to eating myself to death. From there on, I backed off, and I quit my kitchen job. Even so, by the time the ship docked at Boston, I had gained back most of my lost weight.

Arriving at the docks in Boston, there was a small greeting party to welcome the returning GIs. We got off the ship and were loaded into waiting busses which took us to a huge Army base on the outskirts of the city. I was amazed at how well organized everything was. All of the KP and chores was done by

German prisoners. There was no waiting in long lines for anything. I was issued a full quota of uniforms, back pay and last a well needed haircut.

One of the first things that I did was to call home. My mother was surprised. She had not received the card mailed from Camp Lucky Strike. She had not heard anything since the War Dept. notified her that I had been liberated. I was able to tell her that I would be home in about two weeks for a two months leave. All returning POW's were given two month's furlough.

The stay at Boston lasted about a week. I thought that I might get a chance to see Joanne, but she was a couple of hundred miles across the state. I never got around to it before I was told I would be shipping out the next day for the West Coast. So I called Joanne and told her of my situation. She was very disappointed. Apparently, my letters to her from my months in England were on the serious side which had given her the idea that we would be seeing much of each other some day. That day was here, and it wasn't happening.

Next day, a bunch of us were loaded aboard nice Pullman cars, with porters, dining car, etc. Very first class. All of us ex-POWs were headed for California. This part of my journey took about three days. The train arrived at Beale Air Force base, near Marysville, about midday. I got off of the train, carrying my duffel bag of clothes, absentmindedly leaving my folder containing my German POW record on the table of the Pullman. I did not miss it until too late. When I went back to get it the porters had already cleaned the car and thrown it out.

I was given six cents a mile to cover the rest of my trip to Van Nuys. But I did not wait for the bus. I walked to the road, stuck out my thumb and got a ride. I traveled all night, arriving in Van Nuys the next morning, June 6th. It was two years, almost to the day, since I was drafted into the Army from this town. I walked the four very familiar blocks from Van Nuys Blvd. to home.

It is funny that I don't remember too much about those first days at home except for meeting Lt. Muskrat's parents. I was home only a couple of days when they came, at my mother's invitation, to talk to me about their only son who was KIA. It was very sad. They were heartbroken and were in hopes that I could give them some information. I had to tell them that I saw him and the bombardier, exit the broken airplane, only seconds before myself. I told them that I had no idea why I lived and those two did not. Jean and Harvey Muskrat stayed at my mother's house overnight, and then departed for their home near Reno.

My mother had plans to get me out of town. She did not want to see me get married. Dottie had moved out from Denver and was living in North Hollywood for the past several months. Mom had arranged for Betty, little Eddie, herself and me, to leave the next day in Betty's Oldsmobile for Chowchilla. This is where Sister Mildred and brother-in-law Sam were raising turkeys and cotton on forty acres of farm land. Mom gave for a reason that they would fatten me up. I guess I believed everything my mother told me in those days, so I went along with the idea. I wanted nothing but my freedom anyway, so I borrowed Betty's car and looked up Dottie. She was living in a nice board and room house, working as a book keeper at one of the aircraft plants. I caught her early in the morning before work. She looked great, but I kept my distance. After we talked for awhile, she said she had met someone else. I told her that I was glad for her because I had to have time to get my feet on the ground, and I wasn't in any mood to get married. She got her engagement ring and gave it back to me. I told her that I would like to see her when I returned from Chowchilla, and she agreed to that.

I returned to my Mom's. From there I went to the boulevard and found a barber shop. I ordered the works--shave, shampoo, and facial massage. When that was over, I began to feel clean again. Then I went home where we packed the car and headed north up old hi-way 99. I did the driving while Betty took care of her baby, Eddie, in the back seat. It felt great to be behind the wheel again, cruising the hi-ways of dear old California. I felt so good about everything that I could have fallen into a bucket of shit and still come up smiling. I could not talk about my experience of the past year. I was very anxious to forget it and whenever someone started asking questions about what happened, I would blurt out something like "we had a wing blown off and had to bail out. We lost half of our crew." I was obviously irritated so that would end the conversation about my combat experience. Many years went by before I could talk about it, and then it was only to people with similar war time experience.

We were rolling along 99, about halfway between Bakersfield and Fresno when my mother looking out to the right saw an airplane nose dive into the ground only about half a mile from the hi-way. I decided I should go have a look as it was open country, and maybe someone would need help. Sure enough, we were the first ones on the scene. The aircraft was an Army, two seat, primary trainer. It was broken in half at the rear cockpit. One pilot was still strapped in that seat. He was very dead as indicated by his green color. The other pilot was thrown clear of the wreck and was lying on his back, near dead but still breathing. His flight suit appeared to be choking him, so I pulled the zipper down and away from his throat. There was nothing else I could do. We waited a few minutes until we heard an ambulance siren, then got back in the car and continued on north to Chowchilla. My Mom and Betty, and myself for that matter, were surprised at what little effect this event had on me. Blood and guts, mine or somebody else's was never my cup of tea. I used to back into the measles shot line so that I would not have to watch the needle penetration. Now here was a situation where I should have been very much pumped up, but instead my adrenaline remained unchanged This was my first experience with NUMBNESS of the mind.

My two weeks at the turkey ranch was very good for me. My sis fixed me hot biscuits and eggs every morning, and I pigged out. There was plenty of turkey as one day a crop-duster working an adjacent farm, came over low and stampeded the turkeys. Several died when they encountered the fence and ended up on the dinner table. Don, my nephew who was now seventeen, was raising a cow, so there was lots of good fresh whole milk and cream. Sam had butchered a cow in the past, so we had plenty of great beef in the freezer locker in town. I was in hog heaven. I was careful not to overdo it like I did on the ship.

Sam had my dad's old Buick. He had torched off the rumble seat and replaced it with a pickup bed. He and I sneaked away a couple of times in that old Buick, over to hi-way 152, where there was a tavern. We had a few beers, and Sam did his best to get me to open up. He had some experience with the Germans and Dutch in the oil fields of Sumatra. He told of how ruthless the natives were treated as helpers on the oil rigs. I couldn't get around to telling him how ruthless us POWs were treated.

I think we were at the ranch in Chowchilla for about a week when my brother-in-law, Ed Marks, and another sailor friend arrived. They were en-route to Alameda Navel base, having completed their training in San Diego, and were now headed for the Pacific combat zone. They stayed overnight at the ranch and early the following morning, Betty and I, Ed and his friend climbed in Ed's Oldsmobile, heading for Alameda Navy station. It was a traumatic time for Betty and Ed, as the war in the Pacific was heating up, and these were their last few hours before Ed would be shipping out. This was one of the terrible facts of wartime, as it seems there are just too many GOOD-BYES. All the time, it's GOOD-BYES!!

Betty, little Eddie, and I returned to the ranch at Chowchilla. We stayed a few more days, and then headed back to Van Nuys. On arrival at home, I learned that my two great high-school buddies, Jack Clark and Jimmy Allison, were home from San Diego for the week end. Both had seen combat in the Pacific.

Home Again"

Left to right

Bill	*Jack*	*Loraine*	*Jimmy*	*?????*	*Rena*	*?????*
Crum	*Clark*	*Starry*	*Allison*		*Saunders*	

We arranged to get together that night and do some celebrating. Jack had a sailor friend with him, and the three of them had connected with old high school girlfriends for dates. Me, I had none but I did not care. The seven of us went to a popular bar/dance place in Sherman Oaks. The place was loaded with girls, and I danced up a storm. It was a great party.

Monday came and all of my friends were gone again. I was feeling pretty jumpy. I just could not sit around the house. My mother was not the kind of company that I needed. I took her to church a couple of times which greatly pleased her but didn't do much for me. My brother-in-law Bob was working as a machinist at Huffaker Auto Parts in North Hollywood. I told him one day that I was pretty antsy and didn't know if I could stand the quiet for six more weeks. He said that they were very short handed in the machine shop, suggesting that I come over and work for a month with him. So that's what I did with about five weeks of my eight week POW furlough.   Most of my friends were still in the Navy and had served in the

Pacific war. Some had weekends off like from San Diego. This was the case with Bud Kissell. When he came home on a Friday, I borrowed Betty's Olds, and Bud and I went hunting. We connected with a couple of chicks at a bar in Hollywood. What a time we had that night. I won't go into details.

Huffakers was an old established auto parts and machine shop. I moved in and worked alongside Bob. He was always a good teacher. I enjoyed the work as I learned. The work kept my mind off of the year past. The owner liked my attitude and told me to look him up when the war was over. There was lots of work as by now, everything on the road was at least three years old. The only problem was getting new parts. Huffaker apparently had a source. His biggest problem was getting help. He only had Bob, one other machinist and I. And he had engines sitting all over waiting their turn for overhaul.

Along about the first of July, my friend Jack was home for the weekend from San Diego. His girlfriend Lorraine fixed me up with an old class mate, Rena. The four of us went out drinking and dancing. The next week end, Jack was home again and had a date with Lorraine. This time I asked Dottie to go out with me. When I went to pick her up, she tried to give me a hard time and almost backed out. I convinced her not to do that. I promised to keep my distance if that's what she wanted. The four of us went out and had a nice evening. I don't remember where we went. I do remember taking her to her residence, saying good night and good bye. We never went out again for Dottie married some months after that.

I started dating Rena pretty regularly, whether Jack and Lorraine were along or not. I was getting in pretty thick with Rena when one night she told me she was married. I about flipped! She went on to tell me that she had gone "Hollywood" after graduating from high school, got to play a couple of bit parts, and married some hot shot actor. It didn't last but a short time. She returned to Van Nuys and was living with her aunt. Her divorce had a year to go to be final. (Lucky for ME)

My two month leave went by pretty fast at the rate I was going, what with working at Huffakers five days a week and going out each weekend. I was to report back to the Santa Monica Mira Mar Hotel, which the AAF had under lease. So it was about August 1st when I checked in. The war in the Pacific was very intense at this time, and the U.S. forces were gearing up for a European style "D Day" invasion of Japan. I did not want any part of it; I could see myself riding the nose turret of a B24 over Tokyo. The Japanese did not participate in the Geneva Convention rules of War, and it was well publicized that bomber crews were executed on the spot of capture, usually by be-heading. NO Way. I told the doc, at the physical, that I still had some dysentery, and that I had some symptoms of ulcers. I wasn't sleeping well, etc.

Most of this was true, if not exaggerated, on account of all the night life. I had in mind the AAF convalescent hospital that was close to home, at Santa Anna. The doc agreed with me that I had some problems, was underweight, and could use some convalescing. So he assigned me to the convalescent facility at Fort George Wright, Spokane, Washington. I was shocked when I heard that. Oh well, that is better than more combat. I picked up my travel papers and returned to Van Nuys. I was to report in to Spokane in ten days.

Some place in this time frame, we heard on the radio about the first atomic bombing of Hiroshima.

I spent the next few days whooping it up to the best of my ability. I figured I would leave on Saturday, August 11. I would hitchhike to Spokane, pocket the travel allowance, and beat the train time anyway. So on Saturday, Rena and I went up in the hills for a picnic, all by ourselves. We were listening to the car radio and heard that the Japanese had surrendered. NO MORE WAR. But here I was, off in the hills, missing all of the big VJ day celebrations. (Victory-Japan, Victory- Europe was VE day)

I decided that there was no big hurry to get to Spokane, so I stayed another day in Van Nuys to celebrate. My mother had been in touch with all of the crew families when we were MIA and POW. Lt. Berthelsen's wife called her to say that they were to report to Miramar Hotel, August 10th, the same day that I was leaving for Spokane. This was another good reason for delaying departure. So I went on Sunday to Santa Monica to look up Lt. Berthelsen. I arrived at the hotel just in time to miss him, for he and his wife had gone out looking for an apartment. I waited around for awhile, and then left a message that I had to leave for Spokane as I was already AWOL. I went back to Van Nuys, picked up my bag, told my mother good bye, had some one drop me off on highway 99 and headed north, destination Spokane.

With the war over, it seemed every car on the road wanted to pick me up. I traveled all night that first night, arriving in Sacramento the next day. In those days, there was 99 East and 99 West. I knew that the West 99 got the majority of the traffic, so I intended to go that route, but in leaving Sacramento, I got a ride going a good distance north on 99 E. It was hot, and I was tired, so I took the first offer that came along. Big mistake. This ride ended up in the orchard country with the only traffic being the local farmers. So I stood beside the road for quite sometime before a fellow in a pick-up truck stopped and said that he was going to a town over on 99W. So I hopped in, we started down the road and I promptly went to sleep, for now it was over thirty hours that I had seen a bed. And it was very hot.

I guess it took about an hour traveling the back roads between the two 99s. The fellow driving the truck woke me when we got to 99W. I grabbed my duffel bag, exited the truck and proceeded to walk across the highway. I stuck out my thumb and had a ride almost immediately in a four door sedan. I climbed in the back seat, and with next-to-no conversation, I started to doze off. It must have been around four in the afternoon because the tree shadows were clear across the road. ACROSS the ROAD and from the RIGHT! That means I am traveling SOUTH! I woke up from my daze and asked the driver to stop the car and let me out. He must have thought I was crazy. I got out, walked back across the high-way again, checked the sun to make sure I was pointed in the right direction and stuck out my thumb.

I arrived in Redding that evening. I was having dinner when an old timer invited me to a table where he and his wife and ten year old daughter were eating. I told them that I was going to Spokane. He said, "see that Buick out there." He pointed to a '39 Buick sedan all loaded down with suitcases and household goods. He went on to say that they were moving to Roseburg Oregon, and he was driving an old pick-up also loaded down. His wife was driving the Buick, but she could not drive at night. So if I wanted a nice long ride, and would drive that Buick, we could make many miles through the night. So I agreed. They bought my dinner, after which we went outside. We climbed into the vehicles and headed north on old 99 again. Only one problem, I was nearing forty some hours without a good night's sleep. There were no freeways; in fact 99 was a tough two lanes all the way. It was tough enough to keep me awake up through two or three A.M. Then when the road straightened out, I felt myself dozing. Then I was abruptly awakened when I put on the brakes to slow down, and the brake pedal went to the floor. NO BRAKES on this Buick. I down shifted to second, then to first, at a nice level stretch of highway. I finally got the car stopped off the side of the road and waited for the pick-up to pull up behind.

I was wide awake now and pretty excited about the brake problem. I told Mr. Smith about it, but he wasn't upset at all, like he had been expecting it. He went back to his truck, brought back a can of motor oil, and proceeded to pour some into the master cylinder of the Buick. I said, "Hey, you can't use motor oil in the brake system." He answered that it would get him home; sure enough, after he filled the master cylinder, I checked the brake pedal, and it felt very normal. So back in the car, and on down the road, no further problem. And I was wide awake now.

The rest of the trip was uneventful. I arrived in Portland this same afternoon, turning east up the Columbia River Highway. I don't remember too much about this part of the trip. I guess that's because each car I climbed into, I would fall asleep. My last ride was with a nice family, moving to I don't know where, but they had a car full. They squeezed me into the front seat with the man's wife in the middle. They woke me at six in the morning, at the front gate to Fort George Wright. I had slept the whole ride, part of the time with my head on the ladies shoulder. I thanked them for the lift, grabbed my bag and headed for the gate. I was only two days late.

The reception barracks was staffed by two very nice nurses. I told them my name and nothing was said about being late. One of the nurses assigned me to a nice bed, all made up just like at a hotel. She pointed out the mess hall in a nearby building. I told her I needed sleep after I got a bite to eat; she said OK. So I went to the mess hall, came back to my bed and went to sleep. I woke up long enough that evening to get another snack then came back and slept through the night. Next morning the nurse was shaking me awake, stating that they were worried something was wrong. I assured them that I was fine now, after sleeping the clock around.

This turned out to be a great place. There were no assigned duties, no calisthenics, and no first Sergeants to give orders. I was assigned to a doctor, but he didn't give any orders. I spent some time with a dentist getting my teeth worked over after two months with out a toothbrush. I got acquainted with a couple of guys and started going into town in the evening.

I got the bug to buy a car, so I went looking. I found a 1940 Chevrolet, two door sedan. It was pretty well beat, but it had a fancy steering wheel with a built in knob. I was sold. I phoned my mother to get into my savings and send me $800 which is what they wanted for the car. That was a couple of hundred more than it cost new, but that's the way it was for the war years. Cars were scarce. Anyway, part of the rehabilitation facilities at the convalescent hospital, was a fully equipped auto shop. They encouraged bringing in your own auto to work on. So that's what I did. The engine needed work. The car had been rear-ended, which mashed in the deck lid. I went right to work on the engine, cleaning it up. One day, I had my head under the car doing something when somebody gave my feet a kick. I came out from under and was super surprised to see Berthelsen and his wife standing there. I was so happy to see him that I gave him a big hug. He was now wearing Captain's bars and said that he had been promoted about the time we were shot down. He also said that since he arrived at the Santa Monica re-assignment center just at the time of the Japanese surrender, the people in charge went ahead and wrote out his discharge. He was a free man again, even though still wearing his uniform. He was in Spokane staying with his wife's parents. When they invited me out to their house for dinner, I accepted, and that evening I drove my new used car out there. I met her mother and father who had a special dinner for the occasion. I think they expected to hear a lot about our combat days, but they didn't hear much from me. Al told a bit about the few moments he spent with the B24 controls. He said there was absolutely no response. He did not know half of the left wing was missing. He said he rang the bail out bell, and I said I did not hear it because I did not wait that long. He said he had nightmares about falling from his parachute because he did not have his leg straps buckled properly. Also, his lovely wife spoke up and said that the War Department had wrongfully notified her of his death. It was some mix-up in paperwork from the interrogation at Camp Lucky Strike. The evening passed, and I said good night and went back to Fort George Wright. I never saw Al again.

The next weekend I decided the car was safe enough to cross the state of Washington to visit my Dad in Seattle. I made it to Seattle with no problem, but then I went looking for his apartment. To this day I can remember the address (510 9th Ave) because I went up and down hills a hundred times looking for that street. When I found the street, I ran out of numbers. And I found that I had no emergency brake to hold me on those hills when I had to stop. I was fit to be tied when I finally found his apartment. What an ordeal.

It had been some three years since I had seen my Dad. We went out to dinner and to a bar later. This was a Navy town and most of the uniformed people were sailors. I felt a little out of place in my Army suntans. Dad introduced me to all of his drinking buddies. At that time in the state of Washington, hard liquor was not served, only beer and wine. So we sat at the bar all night, drinking beer, then walked to his place when closing time came. Not too exciting for me. I never did care for a bar or tavern unless there was dancing. In fact, one night my Dad and I were sitting at this horse-shoe shaped bar while Dad was shooting the breeze with a friend. I noticed this old geezer across from us, watching me. I didn't think too much about it until I walked around to his side of the room to visit the men's room. This old man got up from his bar stool, followed me into the restroom and started propositioning me. I was so pissed that it was all that I could do to keep from slugging him. I walked from the restroom, back to my bar stool beside my Dad. Then as I watched this old queer, he approached all of the young men going to the restroom. The closer it got to closing time, the more desperate he became.

The next day, Dad and I drove around Seattle for awhile, him showing me some of the sights. I had never been there before. He was employed at the Seattle Post Intelligencer, newspaper, as the head maintenance electrician. He had to go to work that evening. When I took him there, I got a tour of the printing presses and all of the machinery involved in printing a newspaper. Then I said goodbye, and I started out for Spokane, back across the state.

That was a long, lonely road those days. Getting over Snoqualmie Pass was the first milestone, then Ellensburg, Yakima and finally miles of desert sagebrush. I hit this at about 2 A.M. and the first problem was a herd of sheep going down the road. They have the right of way. I was creeping through them, going at a snail's pace when I noticed my engine getting hot and my headlights getting dim. I pulled off the road to let the sheep go by before getting out of the car. I opened the hood to find that the generator had locked up. Since the drive belt is common with the water pump and fan, they were not turning. Man, what a place to be stranded. I loosened the generator enough so that the belt slipped on the stuck pulley; therefore allowing the fan and water pump to do their job. Somehow, I made it back to civilization but it was a long night.

Back at the auto shop, I decided I better do some major work on this old Chevy if I was ever to make it home in it. Apparently I would have plenty of time because my service records were still in the MIA category, and they had to be found before I could get discharged. So I spent the next week working on that car. I pulled the head and did a valve job. I replaced this and that as needed. I pulled the pan off and cleaned all of the oil passages. I should have done a ring job at this point, but there was the problem of getting parts. I put it back together figuring that if it burned too much oil, I would get home and then put in new rings. The instructor at the shop told me that it was a mistake to do a valve job on an engine with that many miles and not do the rings. He was very correct, as I was to learn on my trip home.

Near the end of September, my paperwork arrived, and I was eager to part company with the Army. I went to see my Doctor who was the only one keeping tabs on my activities. I told him that my records were all in order. As soon as he signed my release, I was a free man again. The Doc said, "You are still some under weight. Come back next week. We will put you on the scales, and if you are up a few pounds, I will sign your release." The next week my appointment was on Saturday, 1 P.M. I told some guys in the barracks my situation, and one of them advised me to stuff myself with bananas and milk for quick pounds. So Saturday morning came. I went to the mess hall and ate a big breakfast, and helped myself to a bunch of bananas and two quarts of milk which I took back to the barracks. I sat on my bunk and proceeded to eat bananas, along with a couple swallows of milk, until I felt one more bite would make me pop. This went on all morning. Then at 1 P.M. I beat it over to the Doc's office and found him waiting for me. He was obviously in a hurry to get through this appointment and get on to the golf course or whatever. I no sooner got in the door when he signed my papers and ushered me back out. NO SCALES!! What a revolting development. I was so full of bananas and milk that I felt like demanding that he put me on the scale. Instead, I went back to my bunk and slept it off. I was pretty miserable.

The next Monday, I went to the headquarters building, received my discharge, and I was out. This was on October 9th, 1945. Twenty eight months donated to WW II. I packed my belongings into my old Chevy and headed for home. Thus, my military career was OVER! I was a free person again, to do what I pleased, whenever I pleased.

CHAPTER X

POST WAR

I would drive home via Seattle to stop and see my Dad. This time I found his apartment with out getting lost. Also I had fixed the emergency brake back at the shop, so the stops on the hills were no problem. I had a new problem at the stop signs. A big cloud of smoke boiled out from under the hood at each stop, almost like the car was on fire. That six cylinder Chevy was burning oil like as if it had no rings on the pistons at all. The next day, I took my Dad to work, and then I went to the local Sears store where I bought a 5 gallon can of motor oil and a pouring can. I stowed these away in the trunk.

I spent a couple of days with my Dad. I remember going to dinner and then to one of his favorite taverns. I was still in uniform but had shed my neck tie and was stopped on the street by two MPs who proceeded to chew me out for the improper uniform. I informed them that I was now a civilian but had nothing else to wear. They said fine but if wearing any part of the uniform, I had to wear it all. So I complied and put my neck tie back on. It was not very exciting for me with my Dad. He introduced me to many people but no girls. I finally told him goodbye, and I took off down highway 99 for home.

I planned to go non-stop, so I picked up a hitch-hiker to relieve me of some of the driving. What I remember most about that trip was the oil consumption. When the gas tank was near empty, I would find a station and fill up with gas. At the same stop, I would get out my oil can from the trunk and put in two quarts, then take off down the highway, driving until the gas gauge read one half. I would then find a wide spot in the road, pull over, get out my oil supply, and put in two more quarts. FOUR quarts of oil per tank of gas, all the way home. And it was not leaking. Other than the oil problem, the trip home was uneventful, and I arrived at good old Van Nuys in about two days.

HOME again, FREEDOM again, the world at PEACE again. What more could a person ask for. I was so happy and thankful to be home again, alive and well, I felt exuberant. I experienced several hang-ups, most of which I still have today. One of those is overeating. I cannot put that starvation experience behind me. Apparently I will carry it to my grave, and it will help me get there. Another is a form of claustrophobia. Each morning I rush to pull the drapes and welcome the day, a hangover from the long nights of crowded barracks with all window shutters closed until a guard came around in the morning to open them. It was like being caged in a dungeon. Another hang up was and is an allergy to guns. There is something about looking down the business end of a rifle, pistol or Tommy gun, that sticks in my mind and won't go away. I feel that in those thirty missions over Germany, I saw enough violent destruction to last me several life-times. I did not have to witness any close up blood and guts sort of warfare; but I watched a B24 come apart, go up in flames, or whatever, at 25,000 feet, and all I could do is pray for the ten men inside and then watch for parachutes. I wanted peace of mind so bad that I could taste it. I wanted desperately to put that year that I spent in Europe behind me and completely out of my mind. And I did just that. But the old subconscious plays some tricks. I absolutely refused to talk about the experience with family or friends.

Soon after my arrival at home, I found myself at Rena's house. We got to going out pretty steadily. In all of my friends, I was the early bird to get home from the service. Jack Clark had gotten married and was still stationed in San Diego. Rena and Jack's new bride were close friends, so we went down there one weekend, and the four of us went to Tijuana. We messed around all day, seeing what there was to see. Jack and Loraine did nothing but argue, so not much fun was had.

I approached brother-in-law Bob, about overhauling my '40 Chevy. He said, "Sure." So, working in his garage in North Hollywood, I pulled the engine, took it to Huffaker, and proceeded to give it a full fledged rebuild. I got Bob to rebore the cylinders and resurface the valves. I took the block and had main bearings poured and line bored. For the help I received at Huffaker, I in turn did some wiring in the office. Huffaker was in the office at the time, and he told me that he would like to hire me. However, his old help would be returning from the service soon, and he owed it to them to keep the jobs open. I told him that I understood, and I would be out of there as soon as I got my engine work done. And that's the way it was, for which I am thankful as I might still be there doing mechanic work.

After completing the auto repairs, I started spending more time with Rena. I was lost, didn't know what to do with myself so I leaned on her. I was living off of my mother, and my bank account was suffering for all of the partying. My old friends were returning, one by one, and each had to celebrate with a night on the town. When Bud Kissell got discharged from the Navy, he had a hot tip on a bar in Hollywood. So he and I headed down there one night all set for a big time. Sure enough, we no sooner sat down in the place and ordered drinks, when Bud winked at a couple of girls who came over to our table. Bud took the best looker, but the one I got was no slouch. We had a few drinks, left the bar and drove to Bud's sister's place which wasn't too far away. His sister was not home, but his brother-in-law was in bed. He got up to let us in. We had some more drinks with him, but since he had to get up the next morning for work, he wanted to get back to bed. This little squirt that I was with was all set to go to bed with him. He showed all of us the way out.

By now it was wee hours in the morning, so we went to a drive-in restaurant and ordered hamburgers. We embarrassed the girl waitress at the car window with our heavy necking, Bud and his lady in the back seat and me in the front with mine. She looked the other way as she wrote our order. After the hamburgers, I followed my girl's directions, driving to their place of residence. Apparently the two of them rented a room together. We pulled up in front of a nice house in a nice looking neighborhood and immediately started some heavy smooching. This girl was hot to trot. Kissell, in the back seat fell asleep, so his girl left the car and went into the house. Soon my lady led me out of the car to the backyard where there was a huge yard swing. We made good use of that couch-like swing. The next thing I knew, it was turning day light and the next door neighbor was banging the back door on his way to work or church or something. I said my good-byes in a hurry and beat it out front to the car. Kissell was still sound asleep. I drove out to the valley, dropped him off at his folk's house in Sherman Oaks, and headed for home and bed. By the time I pulled the car into my mother's back yard, it was full daylight. Quite a night.

Another similar episode occurred when my buddy Ken Woodmansee came home after a couple of years in the Pacific assigned to an air/sea rescue boat. His duty was rescuing downed airmen while dodging the Japanese. Any way, he arrived home after being discharged, and he was debating his future with a girl that he had met while stationed at Stockton, before going to the Pacific war zone. He needed someone to talk to because I remember him saying something about being in love. We decided to hang one on and talk it over. We went to a dance place on Ventura Blvd. This place was jumping. Mind you, the date was only a month or so after the war's end. Demobilization was only just getting started. Men were still outnumbered ten to one. In no time at this dine/dance/bar we were in with a couple of girls, and old Ken had forgotten all about wondering if he was really in love with a girl clear up in Stockton. As the evening wore on, I learned that I was partying with a married girl whose mate was still overseas someplace. She was here with relatives of his, and they were not about to let her have too good a time. So when closing time came, Ken and his girl climbed in the back seat of my car with me making like the chauffeur. We headed for a coffee shop on Van Nuys Blvd. Arriving there I heard some heavy breathing coming from the back, so I just got out and went in the all night diner. I had pie and coffee, read the paper, and messed around as long as I could, paid my bill and went out to the car. The windows were all steamed up so badly, I couldn't see inside. I debated what to do, but it was by now early A.M. I was tired, so I opened the door and climbed behind the wheel. Ken in the back, came up panting hard and said "Hey, Crum, (pant pant) Don-cha want another cup of coffee?? (pant pant)" I about split laughing, but I managed to tell him that I was driving me home. He could use my car to take his girl home or wherever and I would pick up the car at his place tomorrow. This idea satisfied the situation. It would have ended there except the next morning I found my car in the backyard where Ken had left it and apparently walked home. This was no problem until I got into the car to go see Rena, glanced in the backseat and find a big mess, pecker tracks all over the place. I called up Ken to read him the riot act! He came right over and helped me shampoo the back seat. I think Ken left for Stockton soon after. I didn't see him again for a couple of years and that was in Stockton when he was married and raising a family.

I wasted a few more months trying to find myself. I guess I expected everything to be like the prewar days, but this was never to be. Nothing would ever be the same. I had done a lot of growing up in those thirty months in the service, and there was no turning back. I finally decided that I better get a job, so I inquired at McWhirters Service Station on Victory Blvd. I was hired on the spot, working the late shift and week ends. I pumped gas, cleaned windshields, checked tires, sold batteries, etc. This was an old time independent with a reputation for their good service. There were usually two of us kept busy at the gas pumps, especially on Saturdays which were still the big shopping day at Van Nuys. I shared the gas pump duties with an old geezer named Ben. He had been employed there for a long time and knew most of the customers. He had a line of BS with most of them. Those that he knew were cranky people; he always managed for me to take care of. But in the evening, after everyone had gone home, I was my own boss, and I spent much of my time in the store, waiting for a customer to come in.

I was happy to be busy again, earning some dollars. Christmas was approaching, and my bank account was looking a little sick. Besides, I was making new friends at the gas station. There was a tall red head that walked by every evening on her way home from work. She started stopping in the store if I wasn't busy and was trying to put the make on me. She told me that she had moved out from the East, got a job in L.A. at Bullocks Dept. Store, rode the street car to and from work. She was renting a room down the street someplace. She made a point of letting me know how lonely she was. And she was beautiful. She must have been six feet tall. But I was going pretty steady with Rena and didn't need another girlfriend at this time.

Christmas came, my first at home in a couple of years. My mother had all of the family for the holidays. I asked Rena over for Christmas dinner. Ed Marks was still out in the Pacific someplace, but Betty and little Eddie were there. Grace was getting a divorce from Fred, so he was not there. Mildred and Sam had sold their ranch at Chowchilla and were now located at Nevada City. Mildred came down without Sam. So we had a pretty good gathering of the family. Mildred presented me with a check, two or three hundred dollars, in return for money that I had sent them from England when they were in trouble with their turkeys. My Aunt Grace and Uncle George were there also. It was a very nice Christmas. My Mom was very happy to have me home.

Soon after Christmas, Rena and I called it quits. One night she asked me why I had never given her an engagement ring. I came back with some dumb answer that she didn't like, so that was the end of that romance. A few days later, I beat it down to the L.A. Bullocks store and looked up the tall red head. I had not seen her walking by the gas station for some time. I found her in the ladies garment department and asked if I could take her to lunch. She was busy with a lady customer, but she managed to tell me that she had married. So that's why she was no longer walking by my gas station. Oh well, win some and lose some.

About this time, I began thinking of taking advantage of the GI Bill that was becoming popular with returning veterans. I made an appointment with a counselor at UCLA. I gathered my high school transcript and made the journey over old Beverly Glen which at this time ran right past the college campus. I did not impress the counselor. He took one look at my high school grades and started talking up trade schools. He suggested Santa Monica City College. This is how I came to get into radio and eventually television work. I do not remember who or what inspired me to make that choice unless it was just the fact that I had had enough grease working on and under cars. Anyway, it turned out to be one of the best decisions that I ever made. I will be forever grateful for the GI Bill which made it possible.

In February, 1946, I enrolled in Mr. Brown's fundamental radio class which was a function of the Santa Monica City College. This resulted in quite a long commute each day, but by now I had most of the bugs worked out of my Chevy, so I didn't mind. I started collecting my $91 month subsistence, and all tuition, materials, and books were paid for by the U.S. It did not take long for me to get very interested, just as I had at aircraft armament systems. I met many new friends, at or near my age, and all involved in learning radio. The course consisted of four hours of class and two hours of lab. Mr. Brown had secured a large supply of surplus radio and radar equipment for demonstration purposes. Some of the aircraft radios I recognized from my military days.

One of the acquaintances that I made in this class was Ted Davis. Ted was an Amateur Radio Operator, or "Ham." Ted drove a Model A which was equipped with two way radio on the two Meter band. We became good friends, so it wasn't long before he had me interested in becoming a ham also. I started practicing Morse code which required sixteen words a minute send and receive, for an FCC amateur license. I found this very difficult, but with Ted's help I gradually worked up speed. It would be several months before I would be confident enough to take the test, however. In the meantime, I hung around with Ted, learning the rules of operating a transmitter on the Amateur bands. The FCC had a lot of clout in those days and all transmitters were monitored, especially the Amateur bands. One of the rules was NO foul language to be put out over the air waves. One of the first things that I said when Ted handed me his microphone to say something to another Ham was some cuss words. Ted was pulling his hair out for he could lose his license.

The spring semester passed very quickly. I was pretty busy, six hours of school, two hours of commuting to school in Santa Monica from Van Nuys, and four hours at the gas station. By now all of my friends were discharged from the service and were home. Five of us got together for a week of camping. We all piled in my car, along with a tent and groceries, heading for Sequoia National Park. This was early in the year for the park because the Winter snow was only recently gone. The bears were just out of hibernation and were very hungry. At dusk each evening, they made the rounds of the camp grounds, checking out each garbage can that was placed along the roadside. Sequoia Park is situated on a mountain side with no level ground, so at dusk began the chorus of the garbage cans rolling down the ravines. Very impressive.

The tent had room for four. Since there were five of us, we decided to draw straws to see who was to sleep outside with the bears. I drew the short straw, so I spread my sleeping bag on the ground beside the big table. I found a big club and placed it beside my sleeping bag. Before retiring, we carefully sorted out the groceries, locking in the car trunk everything except the canned foods. Those we thought were safe, so we left them out on the table. We went to bed believing our food was safe. I wasn't worried for these were brown bears which did not bother people if people didn't bother them. So we all turned in and I slept like a rock. In the morning, I awoke to bright sunshine and it was chaos in our camp. Our canned foods were scattered all over the ground. Each can had been penetrated by a set of big teeth. The vegetable cans were intact, only punctured. There were a couple of tuna cans which were flattened, no longer resembling a can, and licked clean. I had slept right through all of this activity. And the bears had carefully avoided disturbing me. The next night, I didn't bother with the club.

Since the bears depleted our groceries, we had to cut our campout short. We started home a couple of days early. Getting down out of the mountains, it was hot and we were pretty crowded in my two door black Chevy. That black paint really soaks up the sun. We were going down a straight stretch of road, just out of the foothills, when we crossed a big irrigation ditch. It looked inviting, so I slammed on the brakes, turned the car around and drove to a dirt road that paralleled the irrigation canal. I drove a short distance down this little road, stopped the car, and we all bailed out. Clothes went flying and the first one in was Jimmy Allison. This canal was about twenty feet across, ten feet deep with sloping cement sides. Jimmy hit that water and immediately wanted out. The water was right off of the melting snows. It was moving fast, so fast that Jim with his feet on the bottom, trying his best to stop, was headed down stream. And there was some sort of dam and spillway about fifty yards ahead. This was not a great swimming hole. Jim had panic written all over his face. The canal sides were too steep for him to climb. How could we rescue him? We needed a rope to throw to him but had none. A couple of the guys ran on top of the embankment, getting several yards ahead of Jimmy, then one dropped down on the slope while the other held his feet. Then when Jimmy reached that point, they were able to join outstretched hands and pull him up the bank. We gave up on the irrigation ditch as this was a near disaster. We proceeded home and arrived safely, hot, dirty and wiser about irrigation canals.

I think it was about the beginning of the summer semester that my old high school crony, Woody Woodmansee came home after being discharged from the Air Force. He brought home with him a bride from Texas. Woody came to see me one evening at my Mom's house, accompanied by Bonnie, his new bride. He had heard about the radio school that I was attending. I gave him all of the information that I knew and told him if he enrolled, we could share the commute. This was to be the beginning of a very long and endearing friendship.

Woody got himself enrolled in the same radio course but with a different instructor since he was one semester behind me. Never the less, we arranged our schedule so that we could share the trip over old Sepulveda Blvd. We decided that I would drive one week, and he the next. Woody was driving a Model A Tudor sedan which was good reliable transportation. However, it was only a few days into his turn when on the way home one evening a Ford delivery truck pulled out of a gas station in front of us, and we plowed into him hard. The Model A almost rolled, throwing me out through the door onto the pavement. I was surprised because it was like there was no door. I fortunately landed on my butt instead of my head. Woody was sprawled out on the seat where I had been sitting. Both of us were only shaken up, as fortunately, the force of the collision was angular, otherwise we both would have gone through the windshield.

Both vehicles ended up in the middle three lanes of Sepulveda. The evening commute traffic was already beginning, so I suggested that we get the wreckage off the road. The other driver was not injured either, so the three of us started pushing.

Woody's Model A had the right front wheel and axle bent, but it would roll. The other car was mangled on the left side, but it also was movable. We got the two of them over to the side of the road and then got together to exchange information. I joined Woody and the other driver just as this guy was saying, "If you want to claim it's my fault, then you never should have moved those vehicles." I blew my stack and called him many nasty names. There was no question in anybody's mind as to whose fault it was as Woody and I were coming down the Blvd. doing about forty miles an hour, when this jerk came barreling out of a gas station right in front of us. It was very lucky that no one was seriously injured. We argued for awhile, I called him some more names, the cops showed up, and didn't say much. I walked over to the gas station that this guy had darted from but "no, no one saw the accident." Apparently, this clown was a regular customer, so they would not witness anything.

Woody and I somehow got home after this little fiasco, and I ended up doing the driving in my '40 Chevy. I think Woody ended up collecting about thirty five bucks for damages to his Model A which is probably all it cost for a junk yard front axle and wheel. Sometime in this area, for whatever reason, Woody and I tore down my Chevy engine at Bob Robinson's garage in North Hollywood. I do not remember what went wrong to cause the overhaul, but I remember we had the head off, pistons out and most every thing else which would come apart. We were several days on the project; and then when we got it back together and started it up, it sounded horrible, like a connecting rod bearing knocking. So back underneath we went, pulled the freshly glued on pan, checking all of the rod bearings. We could not find anything wrong on the bottom side. I called in Bob for consultation, but he listened to the knock and could not guess what it might be. So Woody and I slept on it for a couple of days. When we returned to Bob's garage, we took the head off of the engine as this was the only place left to look for the knock. Sure enough, in one of the cylinders, lying on top of a piston, there was a hammered piece of steel about a quarter inch long. It looked like it had been a piece of a nail. Somehow, it had got into that cylinder during assembly, resulting in all of this extra work trying to find it. Anyway, after re-assembly the second time, it worked fine. And we went on driving it to Santa Monica and back.

I met another friend at school. His name was Ralph McElroy. We became quite good friends. He lived in Venice at his aunt and uncle's house. His mother was there in the same house temporarily. In fact as I learned later, the whole arrangement was temporary as the aunt and uncle were planning to move to Oregon in the near future. This meant that Ralph and his mother had to find a new place to live. The mother, whom everybody called Vera, was pretty much of an invalid and wanted to join her spouse who was prospecting for gold someplace in Arizona. I volunteered my Chevy for transportation if they would buy the gas. We had a week or so off from school, summer vacation I guess it was; so one morning early, we loaded Vera and her baggage into the car and headed for Arizona. Ralph's older brother Durwood went along. We traveled all night, arriving at this old ghost town early in the morning. Ralph's stepfather, a retired Army Colonel, was not too thrilled to see us, especially his wife. She made a dash for his bed, claiming the trip had done her in.

The Colonel got the three of us a room in this old boarding house where he was staying. It was a real old timer, but it did have indoor plumbing, and they did serve good meals in a huge old fashioned dining room. Outside, the old hitching rails were still in place on the dirt street. The wild burrows wandered through town like they owned the place.

We decided to stay a couple of days to see the sights. Early the first morning, we were awakened by the donkeys HEE-HAW. They seemed to be the town alarm clock. We had breakfast in the dining room, went outside and down the street to where the donkeys had gathered. The three of us took turns trying to ride these critters. It was no problem getting on, but then just trying to get them to move was a problem. They were very stubborn, with no sense of humor. Sometimes one would get ambitious enough to try to buck off the rider, and that was fun. But for the most part, they just stood there trying to ignore our presence. We soon gave this up, climbed into the car and drove a few miles out in the desert to an Indian burial ground. This consisted of a mound of dirt of about fifteen square yards. It had been pretty well explored over the years; but we tried our luck anyway, looking for arrowheads, beads or whatever. All that I found was some pieces of broken pottery.

Ralph had two cousins who lived nearby in this wild country. The second day, we picked them up and drove, following their directions, to some Indian cliff dwellings. This turned out to be an all day excursion for it must have been fifty miles or so, one way, with much of it on dirt roads. The cliff dwellings were very interesting as I remembered studying about the Pueblo Indians back in grade school. We climbed the ladders up the cliff into the ancient dwellings, really having a great time. We returned back to the boarding house in the evening.

The next morning, Ralph, Durwood, and I, said goodbye to Vera and the Colonel, and headed for home. I don't remember anything about the trip, so it must have been uneventful. Arriving in Venice, Ralph suggested that we pool our resources and find a place to live. He would soon be put out from his Uncle's house, and I was getting tired of my commute, Van Nuys to Santa Monica. Besides, my mother was getting to me. I was getting wise to her, chasing off my girlfriends. So

Ralph and I agreed to meet on the following Saturday, to scout around finding out what might be available. Housing was still in very short supply, a hangover from the war years. Rent controls were still in effect. I didn't know what to expect, but I told my Mom that I was taking a room in Santa Monica to save the drive. I also told Woody about my plans, and he immediately said "include me." He and his new bride, Bonnie, were living at his folks house, and it was pretty crowded. So when Saturday came, Woody and I drove to Venice to pick up Ralph. Ralph was armed with the local want ads, and we started making calls. We connected with this lady that was renting rooms in a house, share the bath and kitchen. Fifty dollars per person, which was the maximum she could charge. That way, she could legally overlook the price controls and get two hundred per month. We drove to look at the place; it turned out to be a decent furnished two bedroom house. Woody's eyes lit up, and he was thinking that if we each chip in fifty bucks a month, we could rent the whole house. We approached the lady with this idea who acted real coy, explaining that she was renting out rooms, not the house. We convinced her that we would not tell on her, so she was happy. We gave her two hundred dollars and started moving in right away. Ralph hunted down his brother, Durwood, who would kick in the fourth fifty bucks. Woody moved Bonnie and himself in, with Bonnie agreeing to be the cook for the four of us. Woody and Bonnie would have one bedroom; Ralph, Durwood, and I would share the other. We would have to take turns at the one bathroom.

Bonnie turned out to be a great asset. She was not only a good cook; she was also a great manager. The four of us put money in the kitty, and Bonnie kept us in groceries. We ate lots of beans and potatoes, but we ate. Woody, Ralph, and I were getting ninety one dollars a month on the GI bill. Durwood took a job in a hardware store, so he was relatively wealthy. In fact he soon bought a '39 Buick.

There were two houses on this lot on Brooks Street. Bonnie got acquainted with the elderly lady that lived in the back house and learned that she was the owner of both houses. The old lady was surprised to learn that we were paying two hundred a month for her front house. She was only getting fifty, so the other lady that we rented from was pocketing one hundred fifty. Woody heard this and started working on the owner lady to deal directly with her and cut out the middle man stuff. It worked. We agreed to do some painting and fixing up. In turn, Mrs. Cobaugh, the owner, would rent directly to us for fifty a month. Everybody was happy except the middleman lady. She lived around the corner and when she learned of our deal she came storming over. She did not have any kind words to say about anybody. She came in the house and pulled down some kitchen curtains that she said were hers. She said that we had not heard the last of her, as she stormed out in a huff. But we were not worried because she was circumventing the rent control laws in charging the two hundred a month. So she better keep quiet. She was not only breaking the law but also gouging four war veterans. She could be in real trouble. We never saw her again.

We started the fall semester at Santa Monica. Ralph, Woody and I decided to work toward an AA degree, so we were spending our evenings doing trigonometry homework. Bonnie was some help in that also. Ralph was also into flying. He spent some time at the nearby Culver City Airport, cleaning, refueling, etc., for flying lessons and the use of an airplane. He had his license, and one day asked if I would like to take a ride. I said that I thought I would. So one day after class, we drove to the airport, climbed into a Cessna, and took off. This was my first time in an aircraft since the C47 ride out of Germany. All went well for awhile. Ralph was confident and handled that Cessna really well. We flew over Venice, at about 6,000 feet. Then Ralph decided to do a little stunting--first a shallow dive and pull up, then a stall and fell into a spin. I took one look at the ground spinning in front of me, and I came UNGLUED. I screamed for him to pull us out, and he wasted no time in doing so. I was terribly shook up. I really panicked. If there was a parachute handy, I might have grabbed it and jumped. We returned to the airfield in silence.

About this time Ralph introduced me to a neighbor of his who lived near his uncle's house. This is when and where I met Marian, my future wife. Ralph and I were talking about double dating. We went to the flower shop on Lincoln Blvd. where Marian worked. There, over the counter, Ralph introduced me and told her of our intentions, a movie, and asked her for me. Somehow, since Marian was busy behind the counter, the conversation was short, but she said yes, so Ralph and I departed. That night when I went to her house to pick her up, she got the surprise of her life because she was expecting Ralph. Oh well, we all went to the movie anyhow and had a good time.

Marian and I hit it off pretty well. I guess I felt it was time to settle down. School was going well, finances were stabilized, and the car was holding up, everything was looking rosy. Maybe one big factor was that I was out from under the influence of my mother. She was still at it though. As an example, she had old friends that lived in Santa Monica. These friends had a daughter about my age, so one week end my dear old Mom made arrangements to visit with them. I was to pick her up at the end of the visit and drive her back to Van Nuys. Of course I was to meet the daughter in the process. My Mom was a sly one, but this time it backfired on her. Because I was unaware of the plot, I asked Marian to accompany me to this house in Santa Monica, pick up my mother and ride out to her home in Van Nuys. So, on arriving at this friend's house in Santa Monica, Marian waited in the car while I went up to the door. The lady let me in, and there was my mother. I was introduced to the daughter, but I said I had friends waiting in the car and needed to get on my way. Mom's face dropped to a frown, but she gathered her belongings and we said our good-byes. I barely got a look at the daughter, and I suspect she was relieved for our quick departure.

About this time, Bonnie had her baby girl. She was named Karen. This added another dimension to the household. It was fun, holding and playing with a baby girl. Woody set up a swing in the living room, and we all took turns swinging Karen. Bonnie had fun, too, explaining to the neighbors which of us was the father.

The months were passing rapidly. Woody and I were taking trig classes at the college, so in addition to the radio class we were pretty busy. In addition, we both were getting more involved in ham radio activities, with an eye on the FCC license, which meant code practice. Also, the radio course graduation requirements included an FCC Second Class Radio-telephone license. So we always had that to study for. But I guess these were my best years. I felt totally involved in living every day. There were no bad days. I never looked back to the previous horrible year in Europe. The one obvious leftover hang up from that year was and still is my eating habits. If I am not very careful, I will gorge myself at the dinner table. I cannot stand to see food wasted, whether it is on my plate or someone else's, or left on the kitchen stove. I find myself devouring it even when I am already full.

Along came Christmas and Marian was still my best girl. I was seeing her every weekend. We were getting along fine; I asked her to our family gathering which this year was held at the Robinson's in North Hollywood. I got Marian a make-up compact and presented it to her. My mother, again at her best, said to Marian and I "Do you remember the first compact you ever gave to a girl?" I could have slugged her. She made it sound like I had given a compact to every girl that I had ever met. Marian tried to laugh it off, but I knew she was hurt. And the compact made no points; I might as well have given her a horse turd.

Back at the house, it was a pretty lean Christmas. Fortunately for us, one of Woody's many brothers was a commercial turkey farmer. He called us several times and informed us that he had a turkey for us, a dead one from a fight with another turkey or something like that. We didn't ask too many questions, we hopped in the car and went to pick it up. I remember the first time this event occurred. We walked in the house with this dead turkey, heated a bucket of hot water and began the process of plucking the feathers off this bird. Hot water poured over the bird loosens the feathers ok, but it also raises one heck of a putrid stink. About half way through, Woody lost his breakfast. I don't think he enjoyed his turkey dinner later that day.

Art, another brother of Woody's, worked in a mortuary. He furnished us with some first class suits. And black shoes which were always of the best quality. We asked no questions about the original owners.

February, 1947 came and a new semester began at Santa Monica. I had already decided that I would like to marry Marian and Valentine's Day would be a good time to pop the question. I consulted with Bonnie and Woody and we decided to have dinner at the Brooks Street house. Bonnie would fix a nice dinner and have Marian over. I went to Van Nuys, took some money from the bank and picked out a ring. I did not give a thought to being turned down.

Valentine's Day came; I went to school as usual. After school, I went to Brooks St and got all spruced up. Ralph and Durwood were there, helping Bonnie. This was to be a big day in my life. I went to Marian's house and picked her up, returning to our house about 6 PM. We had a few beers, sat down to the table and enjoyed Bonnie's great dinner. When all were done, I pulled out the ring, didn't say a word, but slipped the ring on Marian's finger. This was quite a surprise for her. Everybody else knew about it before hand. I don't remember what was said.

About 9 PM, Marian and I went to her house where a small family gathering was going on. Marian flashed her ring, first to her mother, and then made the rounds. For the most part, their mouths dropped open. They were all quite surprised. Shocked might be a better word for it, but there was much laughter and joy expressed, for which I was happy. Marian and I said our good night's and went out to my car and engaged in some heavy smooching. A short period went by, and then we were surprised to see her Mother and Dad at the window. They wanted to express their congratulations.

Sometime in late February, someone organized a trip to the snow at Big Bear. Tom Russell had access to his cousin's cabin where we could spend the night, toboggan the next day, and then return home. Mrs. Russell would be there to chaperone those of us who were not married. In fact, Bonnie and Woody were the only ones who were married.

I asked my buddy Jack to go, and Marian got her sister Shirley to accompany Jack. So there were six of us crowed into my 40 Chevy so it was pretty cozy. Some place along the route, we met the Russell's and followed them on up to Big Bear, arriving there at about 11PM. That's when the trouble began. It was raining. There was about one foot of very wet snow —slush—on the ground. And Tommy could not find the trail to the cabin. So we sloshed around for an hour looking for the cabin. Everybody was getting very wet, cold and hungry. Somebody stepped through the snow into a creek and had to be helped out. What a calamity. It reminded me of some of the hardships endured as a POW.

We finally located the cabin and got inside out of the rain. There was little else to be happy about. The cabin had not been used in weeks, maybe months. It was as cold inside as it was outside. And guess what, the plumbing, including the toilets, were frozen solid. Any food that had been carried from the car was soaked, as were the sleeping bags. And no Mrs. Russell. Six of us, Marian and I, Bonnie and Woody, Jack and Shirley, found a huge bed, with blankets, and we all jumped in and cuddled. We finally got warm. It must have been 5 AM as it was soon getting light outside but we stayed under those covers until somebody got some dry fire wood and warmed the place up. By then it was 10 AM, before we were brave enough to face the world.

It was then that we discovered that there was no food in the house. Mrs. Russell showed up, and she didn't bring anything. Somebody had some candy bars which we divided up.

It had quit raining so we decided to go outside and get in some fun in the snow as we were fast running out of time. We only had a few hours left until we would have to start home. So we went out and threw a few snowballs. But the snow was total slush. It did not take long to get wet and cold again so we gathered our crowd and headed for the car which was parked on the road about a half mile away.

It did not take long to get down the road and out of the snow. Soon we were on a straight stretch, and going 60 mph. There was a horrible bang and then vibration. I thought maybe the whole engine blew. I shut it down and coasted to the roadside. I got out and 0pened the hood. There was plenty of steam coming up from someplace in the vicinity of the radiator. Then I saw what had happened. A fan blade had broken off, was thrown down with enough velocity to chop a hole in the bottom radiator hose. The solution: I got out an end wrench, took the remaining fan blades off, and then wrapped some tape around the hose. We scrounged some water from somewhere, jumped back in the car and took off for the Russell's cousins at Fontana.

Somehow, Mrs. Russell was already there when we arrived.. We gathered in the living room for awhile. There must have been about 10 people, Mrs. Henry and some of the cousins. Mrs. Russell embarrassed me by telling how they prayed for me when I was MIA/POW. As always, I clammed up.

After fixing the radiator hose, we started down the road again. Soon it was dark and turning on the lights, with all of the weight in the back (four people) the headlights were pointed high. Every time we met another car, they started blinking at us. Woody took over the driving, and when going down Santa Monica Blvd, Almost home, we met a cop car. He turned around and pulled us over because of our headlight problem. Woody pleaded not guilty to not switching to low beams and demonstrated the problem. The cop let us off.

The weeks sailed by. Marian and I had decided on August 30th for a wedding date. We also decided—mostly me----on taking the Weier's tear drop trailer and going on a two week honeymoon to Yosemite, Tahoe and any other place along the way. So we started making plans. I had a sturdy trailer hitch put on my car. I was one busy, happy person. I never looked back.

I met a new friend at the tech school, Ted Davis, who was an established ham radio operator. I started going to his place after school and learning the finer points of Amateur Radio. He helped me with code practice, also preparation for the written exam. I helped him build a 30 foot wood tower to support a 10 meter beam. Woody, myself and Ted, spent many Saturdays prowling the Amy surplus and amateur radio stores. The military equipment, from the ships and aircraft that were being scrapped, was now being sold for next to nothing. Some of it was priceless. I bought a BC 348 multiband radio receiver, which was the standard for all of the Air Force bombers, for $ 50. It probably cost the government $ 500.

By April, Woody and I felt confident enough for the Amateur Radio License test. So one day we took off from school, drove to downtown Los Angeles to the Federal Bldg and the FCC office. There were 5 or 6 others in the office taking license exams. We were given headsets and paper, were told to sit at a desk, listen to the dots and dashes coming through the headset at 16 words per minute. It had to be written out as it came. It was a struggle but each of us passed. We drove home feeling great.

A couple of weeks went by and the license came in the mail, assigning me call the letters W6BYD. Now I was a real HAM. I started building a 10 meter transmitter to put in the car. I bought a surplus 12 volt dynamotor and wired it into my Chevy. I built a 10 meter converter and connected it to the standard broadcast radio. Then I mounted an 8 ft whip antenna on the rear bumper. Then came the transmitter. I built a 50 watt job on a 10 by 12 inch chassis, using surplus VHF tubes, connected the dynamotor, a push to talk microphone and the antenna and I was in business. At the first opportunity, Ted Davis and I headed for a hilltop to see how far we could get. "CQ, CQ, CQ. This is W6BYD calling CQ". This was repeated several times before we finally got somebody to answer. Then the car battery went dead. That big surplus dynamotor really sucked the current.

One day in May, I went to see the Delkeners, who lived in Santa Monica. They were old family friends from Van Nuys. I don't know how long my folks had known them but they had a big family, all girls and one boy, very much like the Crum family. The one boy was my age and they called him Sonny. They had a farm a few miles out of Van Nuys and the kids rode the bus to and from school. Once, when in grammar school, I rode the bus home with Sonny and stayed all night. Sonny was a sports nut and in the afternoon we played tackle football in a freshly plowed field. That was tough going. I never played football again.

In the post war years, Sonny was going to college on the GI Bill, like most of the rest of us veterans. He was driving a 34 Ford and it was giving him trouble. The clutch was slipping badly. I told him that in my pre-war days, I had changed many clutches on my 34 Ford and I would be glad to help him fix his. So we arranged a day, he was to collect the necessary parts, and I would bring my tools. On the appointed day we got the job done in a few hours and Sonny was very grateful to me for getting his transportation back in shape. That evening, I had dinner with the family. It was quiet, only Mom and Pop, and son lived at home these days; all of the girls had married off. Pop Delkener tried to get me to talk about my MIA/POW experience but as always, I clammed up.

June came and went. Marian and I started making plans for the wedding. My mother got in the act and she pressured the Weier's to have the wedding at the Little Brown Church in North Hollywood, and the reception at the Robinsons which was a short distance from the church. Marian had no objections and I sure didn't. I didn't have much interest in weddings, even my own. I was more for going to Las Vegas to get it done. But I went along with the planning, which turned out to be 95 percent my mothers.

One Sunday, Marian and I took Mom and Pop Weier, in my car, out to the Valley to show them the church. I was sailing along Victory Blvd. headed for the church, came to the intersection of Woodman and Victory and I slowed down slightly for the dip that I knew was there. From the back seat I hear very loud, "HEY, THAT WAS A STOP THAT YOU JUST WENT THROUGH". Sure enough, I looked back in the mirror and other cars were stopping. The city had slipped in a new four way stop.

Our wedding day arrived, August 30, 1947. This was also Labor Day weekend. We had planned it that way to have the few extra days for our honeymoon. In the afternoon, I went to my future in laws house, hitched the teardrop trailer to my car, made up the bed, stocked up the ice box with plenty of ice, beer, groceries, etc. Mom Weier fried up a big bucket of chicken for us to take and I found a place for it. When all of those preparations were complete, I proceeded to the gas station, tanked up, then to Jack Weier's welding shop. I backed the car and trailer into the garage, closed and locked the big doors. I wanted to avoid any tin cans, just married signs or any of the usual pranks that go along with a honeymoon departure.

At my mother's house in Van Nuys, I put on my suit and tie and when the time arrived, my sister Betty, brother in law Ed, in their car drove to THE LITTLE BROWN CHURCH OF THE VALLEY. The Reverend Wells was to perform the ceremony but he was feeling ill and almost begged off.

But by the time everybody arrived and was seated, he decided to go ahead. Jack Clark was my best man, and Bonnie Kroon was Marian's maid of honor. Everything went off perfect. Marian came down the aisle looking perfect. Marians Dad stood up through Reverend Wells' long talk, then when told by the Reverend that he could sit down, he sighed in relief and said "thank you" One could never tell that the Reverend was not feeling well for it seemed that he talked on and on. Finally, it was concluded with" you may kiss the bride." I was a married man.

The reception was held at my sister Helen's house in North Hollywood. Actually, it was the back yard for it was a great summer evening. It was a great party. All of my friends and family was present and everybody was having a great time. The only one missing was little sister, Jeannie. I was so happy and thank full to be here all in one piece, and now married, I was bubbling over.

In February, 1948, I finished at City College and went to work for RCA Service Co. in the brand new field of television. This is where I spent the next fifteen years, ending up as Service Manager at Seattle, Washington. My PTSD showed its ugly head a few times there when dealing with obnoxious customers. It was becoming a problem at home also. Marian and kids suffered as I became numb to the many problems of raising a family. I did not get fired but was pressured to leave. That's when I connected with my old high School friend, "Woody" Woodmansee, at Lockheed Missiles and Space Co, Sunnyvale, Calif.

By this time, 1961, Marian and I had been married fifteen years, having four great kids, two boys and two girls. We had a home in Bellevue, Washington. With the help of Woody, Lockheed Missiles and Space Co. on the phone offered me a salary increase along with moving expenses to relocate my family to Sunnyvale, California, to join the "space race." I accepted, resigned my RCA job and began the move to **Sunnyvale,** Arriving there February 1st, 1962. There I became a test conductor for the Air Force Agena, an early space vehicle. That project lasted six years, and built in excess of one hundred successful orbiting vehicles. When the money ran out for these, I moved to the development of the Navy Polaris, Poseidon and Trident missile systems. I became an expert in trouble shooting these systems, traveling to the submarine facilities on the East Coast and Scotland. I also spent a year working on the Hubble Space Telescope. And last but not least, I spent some years on super-secret Air Force projects. All total, 25 years with Lockheed. I retired in October of 1987.

All of those working years while my children were growing up, I was very engrossed in my work. I spent many months working the "swing shift" and even graveyard. I became pretty much of a "workaholic." My family suffered, but I was numb and happy.

FOOTNOTE

REEDOM!! My favorite songs, "Don't Fence ME IN" and "Oh what a beautiful MORNING." And sometimes, unconsciously, I used to find myself whistling the German marching song the fifty guards bellowed out every morning as they marched up the hill to Dulag Luft prison from the town below. It was a beautiful scene had the circumstances been different.

Subsequent to my discharge from the Army, I was a lost soul for several months. I wanted desperately to put the war experience out of my mind, the whole twenty-eight months of it--even the two girl friends that I had grown very fond of, Dottie in Denver and Joanne in Spingfield, Mass. I turned them off like they had never existed. This was very cold turkey. In their place I took up with an old high school acquaintance. We dated for several months, but I could not find myself. It was like as if I was dead inside. Lucky for me, this girl had been married and divorced, and had to wait for the year to pass to make it legal before remarrying. There was a great deal of partying, drinking and all that goes with it. That went on for about six months; finally she had enough of my PTSD and ended our romance.

The GI Bill was my salvation as it inspired me to get more education. Now it is the fall/Winter period of my life. Since retiring and joining into some of the WW II veteran groups, especially a group of ex POWs, I have been able to loosen up and talk of my nasty traumatic experience. We all shared more or less the same deadly combat, being blown out of the sky, captured, called flieger-terrorists and Chicago gungsters, murderers. Then came captivity, with all of the freezing temperatures and no heat, lice, starvation, filth, boxcar train trips, month long walks with dysentery all of the way. PTSD, you bet!! And I still cannot share these bad times with my kids. I hope to some day finish this book and get them interested before I expire. They might have a question or two.

I have been over twenty years, on and off, writing about this much of my life, 1925 through about 1962. When I began, my audience was intended to be my family, my high school friends,   Sometime in the future, I hope to add some chapters covering subsequent years, my married life and raising four kids.

Until then, this is the END.

HAVE A NICE DAY!!!!